About the Author

K. Alamgeer is a writer, author, and storyteller who specializes in crafting fiction and thrilling stories. Born on the first of August in a medium farmer family in Uttar Pradesh, after graduating from Jamia Millia Islamia University, Delhi, he started his career in the Indian automobile industry as a machine design engineer in an Indo-German auto component manufacturing facility. After holding top responsibilities there for a few years, he started his own automobile equipment manufacturing company to supply engineering machines and manufacturing facilities to automobile industries as well as electronic industries with a team of engineers.

K. Alamgeer

Walking with God

Olympia Publishers
London

www.olympiapublishers.com
OLYMPIA PAPERBACK EDITION

Copyright © K. Alamgeer 2024

The right of K. Alamgeer to be identified as author of
this work has been asserted in accordance with sections 77 and 78 of
the Copyright, Designs and Patents Act 1988.

All Rights Reserved

No reproduction, copy or transmission of this publication
may be made without written permission.
No paragraph of this publication may be reproduced,
copied or transmitted save with the written permission of the publisher,
or in accordance with the provisions
of the Copyright Act 1956 (as amended).

Any person who commits any unauthorised act in relation to
this publication may be liable to criminal
prosecution and civil claims for damage.

A CIP catalogue record for this title is
available from the British Library.

ISBN: 978-1-80439-608-7

This is a work of fiction.
Names, characters, places and incidents originate from the writer's
imagination. Any resemblance to actual persons, living or dead, is
purely coincidental.

First Published in 2024

Olympia Publishers
Tallis House
2 Tallis Street
London
EC4Y 0AB

Printed in Great Britain

Introduction

This book by Shri K Alamgeer is a book that needs to be read with the eyes of the mind. This is a book written in the historical background of a king who transcends all the limits of humanity in order to fulfill his personal objectives. In today's situation, this book becomes even more relevant, which gives a clear message that injustice does not last long. And whenever someone has exceeded the limits of injustice, then a Messiah comes and chops off the shackles of that injustice.

The style of the book is interesting, and it can reach its prescribed message simply and easily to the common reader. The author has chosen a topic on which very little content is available.

The presented book will prove useful in informing the general readers about the information related to ancient Egypt and the goals whose information has not yet been available to the general public on this esoteric subject. The book presented is an incomparable and serious attempt to present the historical, social, and political background of the rule of the great Pharaoh of ancient Egypt and Prophet Moses and mention the activities of his life on which many books written are not found.

The author has done a lot of research to authenticate the historical background of this book. This is a book written for the common people, which will prove to be enlightening and beneficial for people of all faiths. The content of the book has been presented by the author in a very interesting way. The book's interestingness can keep the reader hooked to the last page

I congratulate Shri K. Alamgeer, the author of the book, and I hope that this book will prove useful to all types of readers, whether it is a researcher or a common reader.

Date – 8 September 2019

G S AWANA
Writer

Preface

The extensive construction projects of ancient Egypt, founded by the Egyptian God-King Pharaoh, have so far been a remarkable technological achievement of human civilization. Today, through archaeological excavations, a lot has been ascertained as to what the construction technology and conditions of those people would have been so that such huge construction projects were carried out, which are still present as wonders to modern civilization.

This book has uncovered pieces of evidence discovered by archeologists in front of readers that describe how the Pharaoh governed. What was his religion, how did he carry out construction projects to cast pyramids and huge temples as part of his extensive construction projects, how were dead bodies preserved inside it and what were their beliefs behind this?

During the ruthless rule of the Pharaoh, among Bani Israel, Prophet Moses is born, who brings his community Bani Israel from Pharaoh slavery to Palestine and establishes a strong foundation of Judaism.

The Jewish race begins with the Prophet Ibrahim. Ibrahim had two sons – Ismail and Isaac. Isaac had Jacob. The other name of Jacob was Israel. Jacob had twelve sons – Reuben, Simon, Levi, Judah, Dan, Naphtali, Gad, Asher, Isaar, Zebulun, Yusuf, and Benjamin.

The descendants of these twelve sons of Jacob became known as the Israelites, who were settled in Egypt during the time of Joseph. His descendants were called Jews in the name of Jacob's son Judah, and his religion became known as 'Judaism.'

Through this imaginative mythological fiction, readers will be aware of the astonishing events of ancient Egypt that took place in Egypt thousands of years ago, between the divine power of an emperor, the great Pharaoh, and Prophet Moses.

Many of the verses of the Holy Quran and their niceties recorded below have greatly helped in writing this historical background book and shed light upon the dates and illustrations associated with the Prophet Moses and the Pharaoh. In the Holy Quran, the details of many events that took place during that period are recorded in clear words. By the way, in the Holy Quran, the names of more than twenty-five prophets and their teachings are mentioned sequentially, but the consistent reference of the name of Prophet Moses is more than all of these: a hundred and thirty-five times.

At the same time, the Holy Bible also helped me to bring the circumstances of that time in venturing into this novel. The details of the movements of that time of the Prophet Moses and Pharaoh are found. In the Holy Bible, the details of a few selected people of the era of Moses and Pharaoh have also come in many open words in many places with their names.

In order to know the fine history of pre-mature circumstances before the time of Moses and the Pharaoh, I got sufficient help from a book written in ancient Egypt, and another book *Mystery of the Pyramids*. In which uncountable pictures, buildings, and photographs even today show the social and political structure of that ancient civilization and the ups and downs of the difficult times of life are known.

I got the inspiration to write something from my brother Muhammad Akhtar (Retired Dy. SP UP Police) who used to sit in our home office for many hours and write. Seeing him, I also felt that I should also try to write something, and I also started writing on my favorite subject, science fiction, continuously. I also got encouragement from him to write from time to time for which I am always thankful to him.

The idea of writing fiction on the title of the *Brutal Ruler of Egypt* came to me at the same time as I was working hard on a science fiction book for a long time. This character clicked with me and after doing some research, I was convinced that I could complete this mythological fiction fast and in a fixed time, and I started working on it for four to six hours daily.

In bringing this mythological fiction to the right pattern and making the story fluent, I got great guidance from my idol Mr. GS Awana (Retired DCP, Delhi Police) who guided me in detail about writing fiction in his home office, and I was able to bring this fiction to the place of publishing. I do not have words to thank him.

For this, I am also grateful to all my family members, without their support, I could never complete this script.

In completing this book, I am also thankful to my brother Mufti Zulfikar Saheb, Masterji Alisher Saheb, who encouraged me greatly while writing this book and kept asking about the success of this fiction from time to time.

I am also thankful to Olympia Publishers for publishing this book, who wrote my script and corrected the shortcomings of grammar, accepted the suggestions, and made the script interesting and fluent for readers. They performed every responsibility associated with this novel with great devotion and enthusiasm and also guided me in between.

01 08 2022

    K. Alamgeer Noida

Pharaoh's Palace

Nearly 3350 years ago, Ramesses II, after his father, Pharaoh Seti, became the king. In the name of Pharaoh, the great, in the vast desert of the Sinai Peninsula and the bank of the world's longest river, the Nile, the north-eastern part of the continent of Africa. He inherited the vast Army of Anubis and King Ahmos's Army, equipped with the spear of Osiris (a divine weapon). After the unification of two kingdoms, Upper Egypt (Ta-Semu) & Lower Egypt (Ta-Mehu) into one centralized kingdom (Abdju), holding a double crown the *Pschent,* a combined form of a white crown (Hedjet) of Upper Egypt and red crown (Desret) of Lower Egypt, laid the foundations of a sophisticated and strong kingdom on the banks of the great River Nile.

The rule of Pharaoh was based on the divine powers of a king who had supernatural divine powers made the existence of Egypt, the basis of an invincible and powerful empire.

Pharaoh was the absolute emperor of the kingdom with full control over its resources, supreme military commander, and head of the state. The administration was in the command of the Vizier, the second in command after the king, who served as the king's representative and coordinator of land surveys, treasury, construction projects, legal systems, and archives. The unbeatable strength and wealth of the Pharaoh were reflected in the collective construction projects of the huge palaces, temples, and great pyramids. The glittering gold palaces of the ridges and the huge statues of divine Gods, and ancestors touching the sky, at the entrance of the palace.

On both sides of the grand entrance way, flanked by towering columns adorned with intricate hieroglyphics and carving depicting the huge statues of the Gods and ancestors of the Pharaoh with the heka-nekhakha (symbol of strength) in their hands, were set up in a row. The walls were adorned with intricate carvings depicting scenes of daily life in ancient Egypt. At the entrance to the great Pharaoh's skyscrapers, ancestors were installed, on which the verdicts were inscribed in hieroglyphics (Egyptian formal script). Temples were the center of the economy. They were not only houses of worship but were also responsible for the collection and storage of the nation's wealth under a system of grain storage and treasury.

Beyond the palaces, near the temples in the vast desert, there was the huge pyramid of an ancient Emperor Khefran with a golden-colored geometric charm. The construction that stand the test of time and be remembered for eternity. The four corners of the tetrahedron pyramid pointed toward the four directions of the geography of the ground, and the focal point above, towards the sky, towards a particular star. Millions of massive square stones were used to construct the pyramids in such a way that the temperature inside the pyramids is always constant and equal to the average temperature of the earth. A bright and divine stone was placed on the top of the pyramid edge, which was spreading sun rays all around. There were also two small pyramids on either side of this huge pyramid of Emperor Khefran, and on its topmost peak, a divine stone was kept from which the rays of the sun were splattered all over.

The east-facing, overlooking the River Nile, the symbol of royalty, mystery, power, and wisdom, a huge statue of the God Hor-e-Akhet, carved out of a single piece of limestone, situated on the west bank of the Nile and stood on a huge white marble platform. The face of this statue was of Emperor Khefran, wearing the garland with the imperial Nemesh and the cobra emblem on it and wearing a necklace of blue gold beetles around the neck. The rest was of reclining lion, stood on a high marble rock with feet forward – protector of dead bodies preserved inside the pyramids and a protector of the land of Egypt from the advancing desert. Build by powerful sorceress who have the ability to manipulate the elements of nature that allow them to control the earth, water, air and fire. They called upon to the earth to lift the massive stone using the power of wind and certain frequencies and vibrations by creating a powerful force field around the structure. After getting divinely powers and massive army resulted in the use of brutal tactics to suppress Israelis to maintain control over them.

Once, due to the persecution of Pharaoh, there was no rain in Egypt for a long time, and then the people of Egypt decided to go to the court of Pharaoh to complain. They gathered and began to complain outside Pharaoh's great house.

It was reported to the Pharaoh.

Pharaoh was seated on his throne made of diamonds and jewels with heka-nekhakha (symbol of the strength of the Pharaoh) adjoining with Queen Isetnofret with royal golden robes. The columns of the white light in the palace castle were illuminated by supernatural light behind the thrones, which were made in such a way that the rays of sun once entered inside these pillars, due to refraction, could not find a way to come out and continue to roam inside these columns. When the rays could not find a way out, they would keep illuminating the pillar through time.

Near the throne, Vizier Haman stood at a distance of twenty-five hands and Amun at a distance of forty hands, holding the

Waz in the hand. Along with these, the other courtiers also stood in white tie according to their status.

People made request.

'O great Pharaoh! You are our greatest God, our patron for a long time, there is no water from the sky; our lives are destroying, and your devotees are in great trouble.'

A thin man came forward and said, 'O Pharaoh! What kind of God you are who does not rain on us? So that we can get rid of these troubles and make your glory in your kingdom.'

Vizier Haman wanted to say something, but the Pharaoh held him by a sign.

Pharaoh said, 'O my community! I definitely rain on you. You all keep your faith in me. After eight days from today, we will go out into the plains of Egypt, and from there on the mountain, we will shower on you. Your everyone must be present on that ground and see the glory of our grace.'

So, on the appointed day, the whole of Egypt gathered in that field to see the Pharaoh's wonder. A flock gathered on that plain of Egypt to see this feat.

On the fixed day, the Pharaoh came out of his palace with a spectacular procession and rode in luxurious chariots, and reached the field of Egypt.

There he ordered, 'All of you wait here, we shall go to the mountain and shall rain on you.'

In this way, Pharaoh led towards that mountain and when he disappeared, he looked back to see if anyone could see him. When he had coined that there was no human near him, he got down from the chariot. Leaving the chariot there, he started climbing that mountain. Ascending, he reached the mouth of a cave and reached inside.

He went inside that cave, took off his crown from his head,

and put it on the ground. He also took off his divine Nemesh from the head and placed it on the ground. The hand bracelets with strong divine powers opened themselves with the sound of a crack and went down into the sand. He broke the necklace of beetles and threw it on the ground.

There were a few clothes left on the body. He entered into a dark cave and sat on the ground on his knees, lifted his hands, and started calling someone.

'O Lord! You are the one who gives birth to everyone. You are the one who gives death to everyone. You made day and night… The sun and the moon are walking on the path you mentioned. Your reach is up to everywhere. Only your spirit is liable for worshiping. One who is from the beginning and will always remain.

'O Lord! I know you very well, you grant everyone's prayer. I ask for a little world in exchange for your graciousness to me. My community is thirsty, only you can give water to my community. If you rain on them today, then my reputation will remain in my community. O Lord of all the universe! Mercy on them.'

In this way, the Pharaoh put their head on the ground.

At that moment, the cave was illuminated with a bright white light. Pharaoh heard a strange sound that would make the listener's heart tremble.

'O Pharaoh! We have heard your cry, and have made the clouds subject to you today, that whichever place you will indicate, they will rain on it. So, remember! When you receive instructions from me, you must not be among those who refuse, otherwise, you will become among those who became losers.'

When that light rose up in the cave, the Pharaoh raised his head and happily ran towards the cave's entrance.

At the entrance of the cave, where he had put his crown and jewels, he noticed that a man with ultra-white articles and clothing, a divine face, and attractive eyes, was present at the mouth of the cave. Seeing him present there, Pharaoh got disturbed and became angry.

The Pharaoh uttered a roar, 'Who are you, who have reached here without an order?'

The man said in a very low voice, 'O Pharaoh! I have a query.'

Pharaoh, 'Is this place appropriate for your query? Go and come to our court.'

Pharaoh stabbed to push the man back with his—.

But What! As the heka-nekhakha touched the person, a terrific current ran in the whole body of Pharaoh, and he fell backward on the ground with a fierce stroke. Fearful and shivering, Pharaoh got up with difficulty and said, 'Well, what is your query?'

Divine-faced man said, 'I have a question. In your regional law, what is the punishment for a slave who is to defend his rearing master?'

Pharaoh gingerly answered, 'In our law, the punishment to a slave who opposes his master is that he should be immersed in Darya-e-Kuljum (Red Sea). Now you go and leave my way.'

Divine-faced man said, 'If you give me this by writing, will it not be a justice from great Pharaoh?'

Pharaoh opposed, 'Well! Where would I find a pen and paper here?'

Instantaneously, divine-faced man offered a very precious pen and a divine paper in front of Pharaoh.

'Take these, they exist!'

Pharaoh was very surprised, looked at the pen and that

precious script paper (Tahrirnama) and wrote despite wanting –

'The punishment for a slave who opposes his rearing master and turns his face on him is that he should be immersed in Darya-e-Kuljum.'

By signature – Pharaoh Ramesses

Now the divine spirit stood there with written indenture, given by the Pharaoh.

In this way, Pharaoh came out of the holy cave with his belongings, and raining clouds were revolving over his head. He rode his chariot and took the path of the field. Clouds were behind his horses.

Reaching the middle of the field, Pharaoh pointed a finger at the clouds, and it started raining from them. Seeing this spectacle of Pharaoh in the field, there was a huge noise among the people of Egypt. People were surprised to see this huge feat of Pharaoh with their own eyes.

Now circumstances were that wherever Pharaoh pointed his finger, on the same place water started pouring. Seeing this feat of Pharaoh, the Egyptians started saying, 'Of course, Pharaoh is very powerful and deedful.'

All Egyptians fell in front of Pharaoh on seeing this deed, Pharaoh and Haman were very happy and went ahead in the field.

On the other side, the Bani Israel were watching all this spectacle while standing in the hot sun. The condition of the Bani Israel was that they were craving a drop of water, and the Egyptians were laughing at their badness.

All Bani Israel were watching these heavy deeds of Pharaoh, then one of the wise men among them said, 'Pharaoh will torture you even more, still there is no harm! After this, you will enter the place of peace and in the peace forever, and if you bow down to the oppression of Pharaoh, then you will always be in hell. So, it is better to be patient and stay on your religion.'

Hearing this, all the groups turned from Pharaoh and engaged in their work. Seeing this amazing feat of Pharaoh, no one paid attention nor prostrated himself in front of Pharaoh.

Pharaoh and Haman made their mouths bitter and became very angry due to their courage and considered this act of Bani Israel as an open disobedience of Pharaoh.

So, in exchange for their discouragement, Haman made Bani Israel be deployed in the heavy construction projects of Egypt, day and night continuously.

Pharaoh's Dream

When Pharaoh Ramesses was wreaking heavy atrocities on Bani Israel, he suddenly started seeing terrible and frightening dreams.

One day while sleeping at his palace, what he saw in his dream that while the colony of slaves was engaged in mass construction projects, a fire broke out, and the storm of that fire reached in the sky and turned into a tornado of fire. It moved forward, destroying every affair in the way. Suddenly, the ground started shaking and the tornado moved forward. Every content and the mansions of the Egyptians on the way were blown away like dry leaves by this deadly fire.

Pharaoh stood at his palace, watching this tornado moving towards him, which had turned now into a shock wave, and carried the affair of everything in front, on its edge. The whole palace of Pharaoh was shaken by this heavy disaster. The statue of Hor-e-Akhet was blown away, like a leaf. Large sculptures outside the palace were shaken by the earthquake and started falling on the ground.

This tornado of fire was now throwing all the broken idols and the pillars of the broken mansion in the air ahead, and all this stuff begun to rain over the palace.

Pharaoh stood atop the palace, with astonished eyes, watching the whole incident. Suddenly, seeing the huge statue of Hor-e-Akhet in front, Pharaoh was horrified.

In an instant, a storm of fire collided with huge strength to the palace, and struck the Pharaoh.

Pharaoh fell loudly on the ground with his bloated breath and sweat staining him.

Darkness gradually decreases, and Pharaoh begins to see all around. Gradually, he realized that he saw a scary dream, which has scared him.

Pharaoh got up and struck an alarm, and shouted, 'Haman...'
Then Haman rushed over to the palace.

Pharaoh said, 'O Haman! I have seen a strange and frightening dream, which has frightened us. I will not be able to sleep till I knew the interpretation of this dream.'

Haman replied, 'O great Pharaoh! The dream which you have seen is just a disturbing dream, which has no credibility.'

Pharaoh, 'Haman! This dream is very strange. We will not have leisure till we get its interpretation.' insisted Pharaoh

Haman replied, 'O great Pharaoh, in the early morning, I will send my messenger to call all the Master Futurists and dream interpreters of your kingdom to attend your court, to interpret this dream.'

In a few days, thousands of Futurists and dream interpreters with different types of shawls, opened hair, wrapped in sand presented in Pharaoh's court.

Pharaoh was seated along with Queen Isetnofret at a high position on the high throne with heka-nekhakha in his hands. There was a pin-drop silence in the court.

Then Haman came forward and interacted with a dream interpreter in a state of confusion.

'What do you all think, why you have been mocked here from all over Egypt? Despite this, the great Pharaoh has seen a dream. What is that dream? And what is its interpretation? And if all of you remain unable to express it right, certainly, it's death ahead.'

Hearing these words of Haman, the faces of predictors and dream interpreters turned pale, and they all became very upset. There was a scary silence in the court.

All the courtiers of Pharaoh, Queen Isetnofret, and everyone else too were looking at those strange predictors and dream interpreters.

Just then, an old man, with a long white elongated beard, eyes sunk in, worn and dirty clothes wrapped on, removing the rest of the interpreters, came forward.

Haman's astonished eyes were on the old man.

Old Futurist stepped forward and spoke in a lighter thin voice, 'O great Pharaoh! We understood, since your dream is very strange, so, we are not ready to describe it right now. We should be given some time so that we can look at the stars and think a little bit and describe what we understand.'

Pharaoh looked into Haman's eyes.

Haman said, 'You are given thirty days… Now go and come with a righteous interpretation.'

In this way, the lives of all predictors came to life and everyone withdrew from Pharaoh's court.

On the outside of Pharaoh's court, the old Futurist said in his slow voice, 'Listen, brothers! Listen to me and be quiet. So silent that my light and weak voice reaches you all. Now the days for eating and drinking have ended, all of you leave your food and drink, take the path of deep forest with me outside Egypt, fall on the feet of your allies, and perform full brain stability so that you have full control on your spirit.'

Now everyone wore thick blanket-kurtas and took the path to the dense forest cave. After reaching there, they illuminated the torch in front of their dread Gods and blew the dust and rubbed their noses in front of these dangerous big-eyed, and scared-faced Gods that they may come in their direction, showing them the way to get out of this trouble and save them from this unknown mystery.

Similarly, when a few days passed, and one day a scared-faced God started to throw fire from its mouth, the cave began to tremble.

Thousands of Futurists and dream interpreters were scared and fell to the ground.

On another side, the old predictor was happy and said to that fire-breathing God, 'O Baal, please, give us the arrow of our hard work if you are happy with our hardcore worship.'

Scared-faced God said with great attrition, 'O my pupil Amen-Nakht! Your days of hard work are over. We will make you happy, and we have brought the thing from the sky for which you were restless. So, go and tell the Pharaoh that it is bad for him and tell him the good news of him being drowned in a great sea.'

Now all of the Futurists and dream interpreters were looking at each other in surprise, but old Amen-Nakht looked happy.

After this, all of the Futurists and dream interpreters got up from the dust and ran towards the Pharaoh's palace. Everyone came to the court of the great Pharaoh.

One of them said in a state of fear, 'O Pharaoh! We have brought that thing for which you were restless!'

Haman, 'Describe it!'

A small team came forward, and the old man from them said, 'O great Pharaoh! You have seen a huge fire from the houses of Bani Israel which has destroyed every content in their way, your community, all the forts and palaces of Egypt, even your palace.'

Saying this, the old man turned back, turning his eyes.

Pharaoh got shocked to hear this and looked at Queen

Isetnofret with surprise.

There was an atmosphere of fear in the whole court.

Then Haman came forward and threatened the old Amen-Nakht –

'These are just and only disturbing dreams. The fortune and prosperity of the great Pharaoh and his powers are much more mighty than this.'

Haman came forward, 'Tell me! What is the interpretation of this dream!'

Old Amen-Nakht in a state of anger with his small and ember-like red eyes turned towards Pharaoh.

'...The interpretation of this dream is that a child will be born in Bani Israel, who will destroy and ruin the Pharaoh and his kingdom.'

Now Pharaoh stood up from his throne and swung. 'O our predictors! You have described the dream perfectly. So you also tell me who his mother is and who the father is... then I will just let him be murdered.'

Amen-Nakht, without fearing, fearlessly said, 'O Pharaoh! We told you what we know, and we know nothing further! You should depute your vizier and other courtiers to travel to your country to get rid of this coming challenge. We are unable to make further statements. We don't know anything further than this.'

Pharaoh mocked all the courtiers and said, 'Does anyone else have any idea how to get out of this impending disaster?'

Then a sensible man in eight white linen holy garments, Torah vestment, sleeveless blue robe, and embroidered apron and with a holy plate Yahweh I front and green eye shadow with black eyeliner, (in his hand was stick of power in other world) came forward. He was the great priest of temples, Amun.

Amun came forward and signed towards all the present courtiers and futurists to leave Pharaoh's court in an instant.

Amun, 'O great Pharaoh! With these interpretations, I get knocked about by the arrival of a prophet.

'When some prophets are born in a community, it is in the books that a star appears in the sky forty days before his mother's ancestry from the father's side.'

(Raising a finger up) 'If it is in Bani Israel, as I have seen them waiting for a prophet, this child is the same, then it is the ill fate of your great kingdom. So, I will appoint the master predictors and astrologists across your country to look into the sky and report to the court when that star is revealed above that community.'

The elder priest continued to say, 'When we come to know on the day that star is revealed, then on the exact fourteenth day, which is the day of his arrival to his mother's stomach, then you should make an arrangement on that day; there should be no man will stay in their house in Egypt and spend the night in the forest, so that the spirit does not come in the mother's stomach with the ancestor of his father, and this work should be done with great intelligence and loyalty.'

Book of the Dead

Amun, 'O great Pharaoh! Why are you so afraid of this dream while you are the owner of such divine forces that can pierce even this high sky? Where are your powers that have been granted since the time of great Osiris and Isis, as they had acquired them from the divine God Ra while Osiris's wicked brother Seth by a conspiracy imprisoned and locked Osiris in a gold coffin and threw it into the River Nile?'

An old scene emerged in the eyes of Amun.

Osiris was once a great king of Egypt. Later, Osiris himself became the most important God of all, the God of fertility and even creation, and as the God of resurrection and everlasting life in the other world. He was a great king who taught his community all the skills of a great civilization, gave them law and religion, and instructed them in every useful art. He became the first monarch of the two lands of Egypt, and was so popular that his wicked brother, Seth, became jealous of him and made a plan to take the throne of Egypt himself.

Seth laid his plan. First, he secretly obtained the measurement of Osiris's body by lifting an impermeable layer from Osiris's sleeping place and called his joiners to make a chest of exactly that size in solid gold, so beautifully ornamented that everyone would want it. Seth organized an event in a great banquet and displayed that beautiful chest to all the guests present.

In the meantime, Seth announced that he would give away

this beautiful solid gold chest to whomever of them that fitted exactly into it. Many present there tried their luck one by one by turn, but that coffin became smaller for someone, as it would have grown up automatically for someone to become tight. Then Osiris, Seth's brother, tried his luck in this game. So, as soon as Osiris stepped into the chest and lay down, he fitted perfectly. Immediately, the solid gold chest mechanically fastened Osiris and automatically the lid of that coffin also came up with a loud sound and closed. Osiris was buried alive in that solid gold chest. Then Seth summoned his loyalists, poured molten lead on as a seal, and threw Osiris with that chest in the River Nile. The gold chest swept across the Nile River towards the Mediterranean Sea. Seth himself ascended to the throne of Osiris.

When Isis heard what had happened, she cut off a lock of her hair as a sign of mourning and wandered Egypt asking if they had seen the chest.

In time, the chest floated to the Mediterranean Sea and was carried by the waves to Byblos in the Nile Delta. Here, it lodged in the branches of a Tamaricaceae tree. Eventually, the tree truk grew around the chest, hiding it completely. After sometime, the King of Byblos passed through the site and saw the tree and found it so fine that he ordered it cut down and fashioned into a pillar to support the roof of his palace.

Isis, mourning the loss of her husband, traveled the entire world searching for the chest. On hearing the story of a tree, she went to Byblos and sat sadly by the side of a well in the king's palace, speaking only to some queen's women who happened to be there for water. On seeing a woman there, she plaited her hair and breathed on them the fragrance that came from her own body.

When the queen heard this, she called her to the palace and was very impressed by her divine powers and appointed her to nurse one of her sons. Isis fed the child by letting him suck her finger instead of her breast.

One night, Isis turned herself into a swallow (Ababeel) and flew around the palace and finally found the pillar. She flew around the pillar and saw the chest laminated in that pillar using her divine powers. One night when the queen stood watching and saw the child aflame with Isis, she cried out. Then Isis explained who she was and asked for the pillar to be given to her. She cut out the pillar and got the chest out, then set sail upon the River Nile in the morning.

Soon, Isis arrived in the desert place of Egypt, she thought she could be alone and was unable to open the solid gold heavy chest. To open this chest, Isis contacted her sister, Nephthys, using her divine powers. Nephthys managed to get a priest from the temple secretly, he opened the chest with a special hexagonal divine key.

The body of Osiris was lying inside it, when Isis touched Osiris' dry lips, she started crying bitterly. Naphthys told Isis that they would together restore the body of Osiris again. Then both of them started chanting by placing the dead body of Osiris on the sacred altar. Then Seth reached there with his army. Seeing this, both Isis and Nephthys hid themselves in the sanctuary of that temple.

Seth recognized the chest and Osiris hacked the body into fourteen parts and scattered them in several places in the River Nile.

Isis set out once more to look for her beloved husband.

Isis and Nephthys reached the River Nile and used their divine powers to retrieve Osiris' dead body pieces from the water inside a most important shrine at Abydos and bound them up with bandages, making the first mummy. During the recovery of various parts of Osiris' body, they found all except the penis which had been eaten by an oxyrhynchus fish in the River Nile. Then Isis replaced the lost penis with a clay model. At this time Isis and Nephthys did not involve anyone else in this campaign.

In the hall inside the shrine of Abydos inside which Egyptian deities were erected with grand sculptures, pictures of the deity Ra and his journey were inscribed on the walls.

After this process, goddess Isis and goddess Nephthys knelt, their arms raised in the posture of worship, and initiated chanting to restore the body of Osiris.

Peri Isidos Kai Osiridos semabehdet Anpu

When the chant begins, a stream of blue rays appears from the top of the shrine. Immediately, a book appears revolving in that light stream. There Isis is provided with the book of death by the God Ra and instructed that on reciting of its midst chapter a dead body can be restored that has been killed by some deception.

When Isis opens the book, a white and blue light propagates in this large chamber. Isis starts reading –

Abdju Herui Nekhen Wadjet Maten Sepres Sepmeh Edfu Amkhent osisidos—

When Isis begins to read the middle canto, Nephthys' hand opens up like the golden wings of a bird.

When Nephthys shakes her wings, it breathes life into him again and Osiris' body takes its original form. Isis is still reading that book aloud. Suddenly, some waves of blue light come from the book of the dead and hug him. Osiris opens his eyes. With this, now this part of the shrine is illuminated with supernatural light.

Everything kept in this entire part of the shrine now becomes clearly visible. This chamber of the shrine was filled with gold statues and treasures. Every corner of the chamber was filled with gold coffins and gold statues. In this way, Isis restored the body of Osiris. Isis and Nephthys were overjoyed.

Then Isis mated with Osiris in a secret chamber and gave birth to a great son, Horus. And when Horus grew up, Osiris trained Horus in the same place of intelligence. Horus grew up and challenged Seth on the battlefield.

And after a fierce battle on the battlefield, Horus defeated Seth and became the king of Upper Egypt and Lower Egypt by holding the crown of both Upper and Lower Egypt on his head and occupying the throne of Egypt.

Battle of Kadesh

In the same place – Pharaoh's court
Amun, 'O great Pharaoh! Where is that *Book of the Dead* from which Isis restored the dead body of her husband God Osiris? Apart from this, you must have gained a lot of divine powers from the great Pharaoh Seti.'

Pharaoh in a state of deep confusion,

'Amun, as far as I remember I have not gained any such divine power from my father, Seti.'

Pharaoh turned his eyes towards the sky, some old incidents began to emerge in his eyes.

He himself (Ramesses) stood with Seti riding on a chariot of battle in *the great plain of Kadesh* with his father the great Seti.

The deity Seti also stood at the forefront of the battle chariot with all the battle equipment. Just behind Seti, the great Army of Anubis, with a large line of dreaded black-faced jackals, queuing up far and wide.

The arms, legs and face, covered with black hair. Some parts of the body were covered with cloth. The mouths were dreaded black-faced jackals. There were shining hard gold shields in their hands and feet. This army was in lakhs in numbers. As far as could be seen, only the army of Anubis was seen. Standing in a queue and eager to fight, this astonishing Army of Anubis stood far behind Seti.

To the right of Seti, Ramesses was posted on their two-horse battle chariot, behind him there were six hundred uniformed soldiers posted on the battle chariot with a strange golden-colored spear in close form and in another hand, a rectangular shield of steel with the royal signs of the deity of Horus and many other birds like beetles and cranes were inscribed. Behind them was almost the same sized Army of King Ahmose, as a ground troop.

On the one hand, there was a small golden spear, a small weapon, and on the other hand a rectangular shield with the sign of Horus which was covering more than half of their body.

On the other side was King Muwatalli of the Hittites with a horned, conical, pointed headdresses with a short tunic above the knee and Hattian shoes turned up at the toes. Holding a lituus (Divine Spear) in his left hand as a symbol of power and an assembly of metal discs worn on the chest, with their battle troops in four divisions to fight against Egypt.

Hittites manufactured advanced iron tools using their connections with the Sumerians, a Mesopotamian empire. The spread of sophisticated technologies was their achievement, they were experimenting with metalworking technology for years, eventually, leading them to discover the smelting process of iron that melts at a higher temperature than copper and tin. All the regional empires had a high demand for steel-iron products.

Hittites worshiped storm Gods. Tahunt was referred to as the Conqueror King of Kummiya, King of Heaven, God of battle and victory against foreign powers. They used Akkadian script to write.

Hittites had been making headway into the Egyptian Empire and causing trouble since the time of King Tutmoses III.

Pharaoh Seti resolved to drive the Hittites from his borders and hoped to gain an advantage by capturing the city of Kadesh, a center of commerce that the Hittites held.

Seti surveyed the scene before him, big battle equipment were drawn by elephants with terrible sounds. In front, hundreds of large-sized pointed arrows were observed moving towards him. One of them was hundreds of cubits in length and hundreds of cubits in width. An equal to the same size, hundreds of arrows were moving towards Seti and Ramesses in the vast desert of Kadesh.

Seti and Ramesses had not yet seen such large arrows. Then Seti took out his visionary device and looked ahead of it, the Army of Archers of Hittites were moving in a sequence like a sharp shield in one hand and an arrow with a sword in one hand, looked like distant arrows. A several hundred squads of such infantry were moving parallel. Infantry stopped a few distances ahead of Seti and Ramesses army.

The throne of Mutwatalli, the king of Hittites was now visible. The throne was made of strong iron with hundreds of wheels inside. The structure of the throne was also very strange. It was the warrior throne of the king of Hittites in which so many mechanical activities were taking place. The king was sitting high on the throne. The throne was now automatically determining their position.

The massive Army of Hittites now came forward in front of Seti and Ramesses at a distance of some two thousand hands. King Mutwatalli saw Anubis's army standing in behind Seti and the well-equipped Army of King Ahmose standing behind Ramesses.

As far as his eyes were going in front of him, a huge Army of Anubis stood behind Seti. Equally, behind the Ramesses, king Ahmose's Army stood disciplined and quiet inline.

King Mutwatalli was observing the strength of the enemy, but not distracted. Just below the king's throne, the middle part was constantly changing its positions.

On the other hand, Anubis's army was distracted from fighting. They were twisting his strange swords in his hands, pushing each other around, and making loud sounds. Seeing this Army of Anubis, a terrible and scary atmosphere was being created on that ground.

On the other side, King Ahmose's army lined up with calm and discipline, holding that divine spear of Osiris in one hand and holding the shield of Horus in the other. In this way, the two armies were standing in front of each other to gauge the strength of each other.

Seti now indicated to attack Anubis's army by hand. Anubis's army, so far too distracted to fight, ran forward, rapidly rotating its weapons. As the Army had just reached the halfway point of the run, a mechanical iron wall fluttered from the front and stood in the way.

Now Anubis's army was just a short distance away from these walls, the pointed sharp arrows from these steel walls came out with lightning speed and intercepted the Army of Anubis. Arrows were coming out of these steel walls in the order that each arrow was targeting each soldier of Anubis's army precisely.

The razor-sharp arrows on Anubis's army were coming in such a way that one arrow would hit the soldier in the chest at the same place and the soldier would collapse there.

Sharp Arrows rained on Anubis's army in such a systematic manner that in a short time, the entire Army of Anubis was destroyed and came to the ground. Seti was greatly enamored by this massive Army of Anubis being smashed like this. Seti and Ramesses were looking at this strange mechanical wall from afar. The fighting was fierce.

This time, Ramesses makes some gestures by raising the

hand, King Ahmose's army descends from their chariots and proceeds down the shield ceremonially with the sound of heavy feet together. When Ramesses holds the golden spear in his right hand and presses it with fingers, the golden spear takes the shape of a long spear on both sides.

King Ahmose also raises his hands together, the golden device of his hand also takes the shape of a semi-lunar spear while making a sound. The army of Ahmose does not rush forward, and in a very disciplined and systematic manner, the spear moves forward by holding the shield and keeping the shield in front.

Then this highly disciplined and aggressive force throws these spears together into the air, then lightning-fast arrows emerge from the iron walls and the army of Ahmose takes on the shield. The spears are moving forward in the air, fluttering. Going forward and clashing with the walls, the wall starts to disintegrate into pieces with a huge explosion.

Then some other devices flew in the air from the side of the Hittites. King Ahmose's army was being attacked with fireballs. The line in which this fireball came, smashed all the soldiers who were in a whole straight line. King Ahmose's army was under severe damage. Arrows were coming from the sky in such large numbers that there was darkness over King Ahmose's army. The forefront of the Army was suffering severe damage.

Now Ramesses, changing his strategy, first threw his spear in the air; where it became a circular rotating ring of many spears and started moving rapidly in the air. The ground Army of King Ahmose also threw their spears into the air in the same way; those also started moving in the air in cylindrical form. As soon as these rotating cylindrical spears went ahead and hit the mechanical walls, these mechanical walls of the Hittites were shattered and disintegrated into distant parts. The parts of these mechanical walls began to damage the Army of Hittites by flying in the air. Then, changing the strategy, Ramesses threw his divine spear toward the sky where Ahmose's Army had hurled their spears towards the sky.

Thousands of spears swung in front of King Ahmose's army, reaching the sky in a cylindrical shape, moving in the opposite direction in groups of two. They started to draw the clouds inside themselves. Now lightning started between these circulating devices. And over there, from the circulating rings, it started raining heavily on the Army of Hittites.

In a short time, the lightning produced by the clouds moved towards the main part of the Army of Hittites fighting below. Now the elephants involved in the military of the Hittites began to face a severe lightning strike. Elephants started fleeing here and there and collapsing on the ground. The rain and lightning were wreaking heavily on the Army of Hittites. The Army was suffering heavy losses. Army equipment was also destroyed by amazing lightning.

The elephants which were running towards King Ahmose's army were targeted by Ramesses and Pharaoh Seti with divine spears. The spear would pass through the elephants and turn around, return to the hands. Hittite soldiers were suffering heavy losses now. There was terrible destruction all around.

The throne of Hittites was still protected from this thunderclap. It was now transformed into a complete fighter throne and rose into the air above the ground. The center of the throne was moving around on its axis continuously. Now a few rays came out of the throne and hit the rotating spears in the sky, then there were fierce explosions between those cylindrical rotating spears, and the whole sky was filled with fire.

The throne of the king of Hittites moved forward in the air and came out of that thunderbolt and arrived over King Ahmose's army. Arrows were raining from the throne at such a rapid pace that King Ahmose's soldiers smashed in a particular area. The Army of King Ahmose was unable to control this mechanical throne in any way.

Seti and Ramesses were both watching this amazing device with great surprise. Now Ramesses drew a bow and golden spear from his chariot and converted it into an arrow and targeted the throne of the king. Just after the arrow came out of the bow, it took a round shape in the sky and started spewing a rain of fire on the throne simultaneously. This caused a fire on the throne, and it started to break. Arrows from the throne now stopped coming at such a rapid speed. The revolving center of the throne now stopped with a loud voice, and that wonderful iron throne of Hittites fell to the ground engulfed in flames.

Ramesses was still watching the mechanical processions in that mechanical throne of King Hittites. After some time, this throne automatically recovered itself and became as it was earlier.

Arrow rain again started on King Ahmose's Army and caused maximum damage to the troops. New mechanical walls were coming in the air and attacking the enemy with their sticking arrows.

Ramesses and the Army of King Ahmose were also counter-attacking in the same way and damaging maximum on another side. But none of the sides looked weaker after a day-long battle.

The Egyptian and Hittite armies were pretty evenly matched in power and technology. Egyptian chariots were faster and had one rider aboard with their divine spear of Osiris and metal shield. Hittite chariots accommodated many fighters with more spears and iron tools stronger than the Egyptians. Hittite military technology was some of the most sophisticated of its time.

Both the armies were fighting with a state of great technology and none of the sides looked defeated after a day-long furious battle. Pharaoh Seti and Ramesses failed to achieve their objective of capturing the king of Hittites, and Mutwatalli retained control of Kadesh; he failed to crush the Egyptians as he hoped to.

Then after a furious clash between Ramesses and King Mutwatali and his whole Army leveled the earth, and Mutwatalli saw the great tribulation, a strange thing happened, a solar eclipse occurred. The Wisemen from the king Mutwatalli interpreted this sign as meaning the Gods did not want this battle to carry on. Pharaoh Seti and Ramesses and the whole Army were also taken aback and got scared for a while on seeing this amazing incident. This incident led to the battle stopping for some time.

The king of Hittites came forward along with their battle throne and said, 'O great Seti! I expect peace from you. I also want great enemies to stop this stalemate.'

Now Ramesses closed his spear, immediately all the Army of King Ahmose also stood together in a straight posture with the sound of their spears closer.

Pharaoh Seti! 'O King Mutwatalli! Your technology was very sophisticated, and your skills were amazing. You had been making headway into the Egyptian Empire and causing troubles for a long time. We drive many times to resolve our borders and hoped to gain an advantage. Now the decision will come today in this plain of Kadesh.'

Mutwatalli! 'O great Seti! I assure you not to cause any harm or trouble to the Egyptian Empire in the near future. The Hittites are skilled in metalwork and can teach the Egyptians how to make superior weapons and tools while the Egyptians, masters of agriculture, can share their knowledge with the Hittites. The two great nations can continue a mutually beneficial relationship. Hittites will send skilled slaves, who will build a city for you in Egypt that will restore your strength.'

Ramesses looks at Seti. Seti and Ramesses agree to this proposal of King Mutwatalli, and this battle of Kadesh ended under the peace treaty between the two countries.

'Pharaoh, the great king, the king of the country of Egypt, shall never attack the country of Hatti to take possession of a part (of this country). And Mutwatalli, the great king, the king of the country of Hatti, shall never attack the country of Egypt to take possession of a part (of that country). Hitti will teach Egyptians to use massive machines to lift the enormous blocks using deferent frequencies and shape the stone in incredible precision.'

A peace treaty were made between Hittites and Egypt. A cylindrical seal was used to sign the treaty documents.

After that, Pharaoh Seti claimed a great victory for Egypt as he had defeated his enemy in the battle of Kadesh.

Mutwatalli also claims his victory, because he didn't lose the city of Kadesh.

The treaty of Kadesh, the first peace treaty in the history of two great civilizations to determine whether or not they were at war with each other.

Seti and Ramesses then return to Egypt. Seti picks up the Book of the Dead from the chariot and a golden hexagonal device in the other hand. Seti pressed the small device; immediately many petals with supernatural light rays became visible.

Pharaoh Seti applied this open golden device to the mark made on the book and turned it aside. In this way, the *Book of the Dead* opened up with divine scintillations around it. Ramesses saw from a distance that Pharaoh Seti was reciting some spell from that book –

'Peri isidos kai Anubis unas Ra.'

Suddenly, that whole Army of Anubis got up from the ground and spreading the dust all around ran behind Pharaoh Seti.

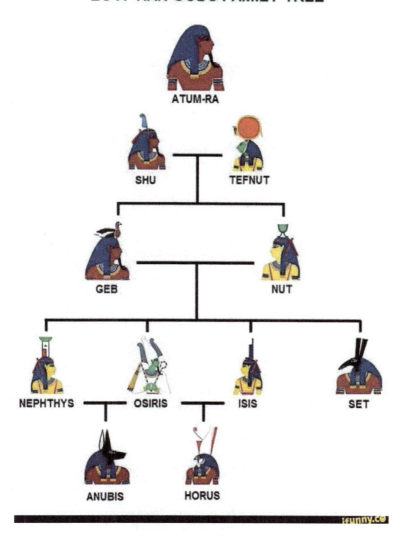

Ancient Egyptian Royal Crown and Symbolic Headdresses

S.NO.	NAME	SYMBOL	SYMBOL SIGN
1	(Hedjet)	White Crown of Upper Egypt	
2	(Deshref)	Red Crown of Lower Egypt	
3	(Pschent)	White & Red Double Crown	
4	(Atef)	Crown of God Osiris	
5	(Heka-Nekhakha)	Sign of Power	
6	(Ankh)	Key to Enter the After Life	
7	(Was)	Sceptre, Symble of Power	
8	(Heb-Sed)	'Royal Jubily Festival after 25 Years Throne	
9	(Amulet)	Divine Protective Device to worn	
10	(Wadjet)	Eye of Horus	
11	(Canopic Jars)	Four sons of Horus	
12	(Anubish)	Guardian, God of Dead and Tomb	

13	(Ta-Semu)	Upper Egypt	
14	(Ta-Mehu)	Lower Egypt	
15	(Hathor)	Isis, Hator Crown	
16	(Nekhen)	God of safeguard and War	
17	(Geb)	Sky God	
18	(Nut)	Earth Goddess	
19	(Khnum)	God of Nile, Water	
20	(Seti)	God of Troops	
21	Atum (Ra)	Sun God, God of Earth & Sky	
21	(Ra)	Crown of God Ra	
22	(Khepri)	Beetles, God of Creation, after life	
23	(Selket)	Scorpion God Of magic and Protection	

Four Sons of Horus

Heb-Sed

Seti arrived in Egypt and announced heb-sed (a state ceremony after twenty-five years of rule).

The ground in front of the Great Pyramid and Khafren's Sheerin was chosen to host heb-sed. Statues with ram's heads were installed in a seated position on each side of the road. Some idols, in the shape of a man's face and a lion's body, were installed in a continuous row set on the golden rocks. Behind them, the statues of the earlier Pharaoh, standing upright, cross-holding Heka and Nekhakha in their hands. Huge pillars were touching the sky, inscribing the history of that time by hieroglyphs.

A throne in a high place for Pharaoh Seti and his queen was established. All the idols and the throne of Pharaoh were shining in golden color.

At the same time, the construction projects of the pyramid on which slaves were working day and night, and the materials to hold construction, were visible from here. Right in front, the Nile River was flowing at its full stream. On both sides of the River Nile, the green dates and figs were pleasing to the eye. Just before the throne, millions of chairs were lined up for the Egyptians to sit.

Pharaoh Seti holding heka-nekhakha in his hands with his entire family group reaches the throne. He is accompanied by Ramesses and his courtiers. When Pharaoh Seti and his queen sit on the throne, a large number of Egyptians also sit in their respective places.

Pharaoh Seti indicates the commencement of the ceremony towards one of the stalwarts standing in line. When the vizier immediately raises one hand forward, the curtain behind the throne disappears somewhere in the air. Just behind the Pharaoh Seti and the throne of the queen, a huge sky-touching golden-colored idol of the sun, God Hor-e-Akhet, becomes visible, and just behind it the huge pyramid of Khafren, with bright divine stone lights on top of it, looking very, very strange. When the Egyptians sitting in front saw this view, all the people became very delighted and praised Pharaoh Seti. Egyptians arise! No doubt, Pharaoh only has such divine power.

Pharaoh Seti declared his son Ramesses here as his successor. The head priest from the temples presented and wore a cobra-headed crown on the head of Ramesses. Ramesses, wearing beads of the royal mark around the neck and necklace of the God Horus, made of gold around the neck, now occupies the throne of the successor.

Now the ceremony of heb-sed began in this wonderful plain. Thousands of dancers performed group dances to the melodious musical sound. From the beginning to the end, all the dancers were performing the same pattern and in the same pose.

Great performance…!

Their interaction was very high. Beautiful dancers were performing enchanting dances to the music in light white clothes. In this sequence, when a very beautiful dancer started dancing on a circled flower with dancing feet and struck the feet over the flower, her wings opened.

As soon as these wings spread all over, precious pearls came out of them and started scattering around them. The shining true pearls spread far and wide. And upon seeing further, many such dancers were creating wonders.

The Egyptian voice and everyone present was cheering. When this spectacular performance ends, there is a buzz around. Pharaoh Seti rises from his throne together.

Pharaoh Seti! 'Would you like something even better?'

Egyptians! 'What can be better than that?'

Pharaoh Seti! 'Better over this is, your Pharaoh's extraordinary skills.'

Pharaoh Seti sits on the throne carrying the Harp and says in the air.

'Ring.' A piece of sweet music resonates in the atmosphere.

The wind comes out among the leaves of trees and emits very sweet music.

The fingers of Pharaoh Seti were falling on the strings of the harp such that honey was dissolving in the ears of the listener.

Egyptians had never heard such sweet music before.

Hearing this, whatever was there, it was frozen there. The assembled dancers from far away were frozen by the magic of this instrument.

The hearts of the listeners were being forgotten. All listeners present there had lost control over themselves.

Kinds of birds flying in the sky came down on the trees to listen to the melody of this music.

The wild animal's feet stopped there. All these phantoms were entwined in the magic of Seti. The flowing water of the River Nile stopped flowing.

Now the music had reached the limit.

The water of the Nile River rose with a big wave and started moving toward this ceremony. The music was still playing.

Egyptians had never heard such sweet music before. Hearing this, whatever was there, it was all frozen there.

The hearts of the listeners were forgetting to beat. The listeners lost control over themselves. The mountain of water of the great River Nile had come over the heads of the gathering.

Now the queen of Pharaoh Seti spreads both her hands and her golden wings. Seeing this divine form of the queen, Egyptians' eyes were torn apart. While the mountain of water was close to drowning people in a broad roar, Pharaoh stopped their hands without looking up and raised his palm toward the water, with immediate effect the mountain of water broke backward.

When the people behind him saw the water inundation, their senses were lost. Seeing this whole circumstance, the vizier and all the courtiers fell in prostration in front of Pharaoh Seti. Seeing this movement, all Egyptians did the same.

After all, when Seti returns to his palaces, all Egypt lean in front of Seti.

When he passes by a construction project, Israel's community engaged in construction projects does not bow down to Seti. And keep watching the King Seti as they stand. The vizier Haman signs them to bow down, but they still don't bow down.

Seti proceeded with anger seeing to Vizier Haman.

Haman ordered the Egyptians to put all of them in the harshest things and double the work over them. Orders released that the stones of the mountain should be washed by their old and pregnant women and before the night was over, the wages should be stored in the royal treasury.

Seti went to sleep in the palace, then at the last portion of the night, lightning struck at the house suddenly. Seti got up instantaneously, and the palace was filled with white light. Due to which Seti's eyes were not fully opened. When Seti looked more vigorously, he found a white-clothed man in front of him.

The white-clothed spirit came a little closer and said, 'What do you think? You have been deceived.'

Despite the strong setbacks, Seti asked, 'Who are you and how did you reach here?'

The white-clothed spirit said, 'I can come anywhere; I have been doing this work since the creation of this earth, and till the time this land is maintained, I will continue to do so. Your journey is over, and now you will see what you have done for a long journey ahead of you.'

And in this way, the eyes of Pharaoh Seti widened.

He could not get up despite using his full strength. But Seti did something by raising his hand slightly on the front wall with his other hand. So, there were some mechanical actions and after complicated actions, some small doors started to open and a small box came out automatically.

On the small box many symbols were inscribed by the picture script, in this box many small drawers were opening one after the other. After all, in an open drawer, a golden-colored shining supernatural geometric-shaped chasm tool was visible. A perfect composition of the efficient construction art of the Egyptians.

Then the one who had come raised their hand over Seti, immediately some blue stripes came out of him and, wrapped in the hand of the spirit, the eyes of Seti were left opened.

Now the incoming spirit hit the instrument that saw a sign to call the viziers in the palace. As the instrument was hit, viziers ran from outside toward the king's palace.

The spirit easily vanished from the walls of the palace and disappeared.

When the viziers and all the courtiers entered this palace, they saw Pharaoh Seti's body was lifeless, eyes opened. Nothing seemed disorganized in the palace.

Seti's viziers, after visualizing Seti's body thoroughly, gave a message to Ramesses that Seti was no longer.

Ramesses glanced at that geometrical-shaped golden key in an open drawer.

Four Sons of Horus

Again in same place
Amun, 'Yes, what you said, O Pharaoh, about the solid geometrical and bright hexagonal device, that is an esoteric mechanical key.

'In the days of the great ruler, Tutankhamun, the divine *Book of the Dead* was stored in a mechanical gold enclosure and that enclosure could be opened only by that esoteric mechanical key. And that esoteric mechanical device was beamed from one ruler to another.

'Only by that divine key, may the *Book of the* Dead be opened. According to the boon of the God Ra, whoever has the key and the *Book of the Dead*, any dead soul can be returned to his body and restored if his whole body is preserved.'

Haman in a hurry, 'O great Pharaoh! you do not need to be afraid of any danger and anyway, you own two large armies, the Army of King Ahmose and the jackal-headed Army of Anubis. And these two forces are unbeatable. You should issue an order now to take Bani Israel at the tip of the sword to close the chapter that any child will be born of Bani Israel.

Amun said, 'O Haman your idea is highly inappropriate. Where would the slaves come for all Pharaoh's great construction project sites in Egypt, if you destroyed all Bani Israel? Remember! Did you notice what that old Futurist Kumejtarash said?'

'Remember, he said that when a prophet is sent to a community, just forty days before his transformation from father back to mother's stomach a holy star will appear in the sky, the kingdom where this star will appear in the sky has the misfortune of that kingdom and its king. His kingdom will be shattered.'

Hearing this analysis of Amun, both Pharaoh and Haman were shocked.

Haman came forward! 'Today I shall appoint all the master futurists and magicians of Egypt to keep an eye on the sky with great vigor, that as soon as that star appears in the sky, then it should be reported in the court of the Pharaoh.

Amun said, 'O great Pharaoh! Now till these futurists and magicians of Egypt inform you about the sky of that star being revealed, you must acquire the *Book of the Dead* with divine power so that the throne of Egypt becomes completely safe.'

Haman, 'O great Pharaoh! Has that divine *Book of the Dead* reached you?'

Pharaoh (on revealing) said, 'O Haman! I had once seen that *Book of the Dead* with supernatural power with my father Seti when the great Seti opened that book and resurrected all the Army of Anubis on the plain of the battle of Kadesh. But I did not get that divine book from the great Seti. Nor did the great Seti ever talk to me about the divine powers of that book. I still don't know where that book is.'

Amun said, 'And those divine keys, that you have just mentioned, when the geometric structure was present in the palace, at the end time of Seti. Where is it?'

Ramesses the great, then remembered back and a scene emerged in his eyes!

When Pharaoh Seti was dead, according to ancient Egyptian beliefs, a complex process of preserving a dead body began for him to enter another world. This process of preserving the dead body was carried out according to the book of the dead, as its procedure was given in full detail in the *Book of the Dead*. They believed that after the death of this body, his life continued to exist. When a king dies, a kind of spiritual double called *ka* continues to exist. Dead king and *ka* went through life together. It also had a sort of external soul called *ba* as a human-headed bird. After death, the *ka* needed a home and *ba* a link with the soul of the dead. In a tomb, the mummy provided a connection between the dead's ba. So, Egyptians built huge tombs or pyramids to rest the soul, and priests and relatives gave offerings of food, drink, and other daily uses to the dead.

In this way, the process of preservation of Seti's dead body began. It was a seventy-day process that was carried out by the chief priests of Egyptian temples. The dead body was handed over to Anubis and taken to the holy place called the pure place.

It was their responsibility to perform rituals in the tomb. Anubis stripped his body and laid it on a tabletop and started with a most expensive method of preservation.

1. The dead body is first cleaned with holy water.
2. By making an incision on the left side of the stomach there, the liver, lungs, and intestines are taken out. The heart is usually kept inside the body. According to the mythological beliefs of Egyptians, the heart is the symbol of all emotion and fame, which is also needed in the afterlife ahead. Through a hook device, the brain from the dead body is also removed through the nose.
3. The entire body and the extracted organs are kept in salt for forty days so that their full moisture is absorbed.
4. These dried organs are wrapped in linen cloth and kept in four separate canopic jars with completely air-resistant lids.
5. The four canopic jars set in a square chest held organs under the protection of the four sons of Horus.

These four jars are prepared in this order

The Four Sons Of Horus				
God	Protects	Head	Point	Goddess
Imsety	Liver	Human	South	Isis
Hapy	Lungs	Baboon	North	Nephthys
Duamutef	Stomach	Jackal	East	Neit
Qebehsenuef	Intestines	Falcon	West	Selkis

6. The dry body is immersed in oil and taken out.
7. The open and cut parts of the body are sealed with wax.
8. Then rings are put on the fingers, bracelets on the wrists, and a large precious stone-carved scarab beetle over the heart.
9. Then they poured heated resin over all the body and began wrapping it with the linen strips. As much as 2000 meters of various widths went into mummy wrapping.
10. A mask of pure gold is placed over the mouth which is a replica of the person who died.
11. Over the body are gilded gems which are worn in the form of protective talisman-like beads, and Heka and Nekhakha made of gold are held in the hand.
12. Now the whole body is closed by placing it in a solid gold coffin on which is painted the scenes and rules of entering the next world, according to the guidelines of the *Book of the*

Dead.

Then the final journey of that coffin starts after seventy days. Which followed the royals, priests, and male relatives of the dead showing their sorrow by their silence and solemn steps as they walked, leaning on their long sticks. Along with this coffin of Pharaoh, his life's necessities are taken toward the pyramids like gold gems, food and drink, and other useful things in life. It was believed that all these things would be used in life after death.

Now placing this coffin on a gold platform, which thirty to forty men take up together, and the jars containing the chest (four sons of Horus) are taken to the pyramid. The rest of the royal family and other courtiers follow this coffin. The coffin reaches the pyramid on passing nearby Hor-e-Akhet. There, they enter the tunnel way, and through the narrow path, the coffin is brought into a large hall of pure white granite. On the white walls of this hall, pictures of the deities Ra, Osiris, Isis, Horus, and many Gods are inscribed.

In one picture, the God Osiris was shown welcoming the Pharaoh with an Ankh (a key to enter the other world). In the second picture, Pharaoh was shown being welcomed by Anubis.

A solid gold coffin is placed on a square of white granite block and there all the royals pay their last offering to the soul.

At last, Amun asked for the last permission from the queen of Pharaoh Seti.

The queen gestured to Amun with a 'yes'. Now Amun rotated a key a little bit by putting it on that square stone, then the square stone opened from the top and the gold coffin went into the stone and the square stone closed again.

Now four canopic jars (sons of Horus) were placed on top of that square stone.

Amun now took out a mechanical key by rotating it in a

circle and then the square stone also took in these four jars. Amun broke the bond that was left in one place by rolling it. So, sand started coming out from there, and the white marble square stone of the coffin entered the floor below.

And the doors through which that royal family entered there began to close. First, the doors of the chamber into which the slaves had carried the coffin of Pharaoh closed automatically.

Those scared slaves were locked inside forever. There was still sand constantly coming out from many places and all the doors were slowly closing. Then the royal family moved out through a fast-closing door and came out of that tunnel way. Many doors went back and forth automatically.

After that, a grand ceremony was held to radiate Ramesses on the throne of Egypt. Behind the Egyptian throne, there were the huge statues of the early Pharaohs, shining brightly; Ramesses and Queen Isetnofret were called forward by chanting priests.

When Ramesses came to the throne, the chief priests of the temples of Amun placed the combined crown (Pschent), the white crown of Upper Egypt (Hedjet), and the red crown of Lower Egypt (Deshret) on the head of Ramesses.

Queen Isetnofret was looking very attractive in the golden shiny clothes and headrest of a cobra, sitting on the throne. Ramesses then awarded Heka and Nekhakha and proclaimed – Pharaoh Ramesses the Great, the king of both states and owner of both armies, the Army of King Ahmose, and the jackal-headed great Army of Anubis.

Ramesses was then given Ankh, which symbolizes both mortal existence and the afterlife. Now, Pharaoh Ramesses, the great, was the chief patron of Egyptian temples. After this, Ramesses wore around the neck an Egyptian royal necklace made of gold beads and blue beads, and some of the divine powers were symbolized by the previous Egyptians. Pharaoh sat on the throne of Egypt and declared! 'I hold Haman as my chief vizier.'

Now, Amun offered Haman the mark of the vizier, Was (the symbol of power). Haman respectfully accepted that sign and bowed, concerning Pharaoh. In this way, the phase of Pharaoh Ramesses the Great began and Haman as a chief vizier in the kingdom.

Haman came down to the throne, raising his hands in a gesture of blessing to the Pharaoh and Queen Isetnofret.

"O Gods of the great land of Nile, O Gods of Amun, who granted passage to the Nile, freedom to Egypt, and strength to the almighty Pharaoh, may all those Gods be declared as the blesses to almighty Pharaoh. O Gods of the land of Egypt, give great strength to our devoted Pharaoh against his enemies. O Gods of the land of Egypt, make Pharaoh the viceroys of the heavenly divine forces that the god Re had once a time, and the divine forces that Osiris and Isis were given, and the prosperity to our sovereign Pharaoh in the land of Egypt."

Queen Hatshepsut's Temple

Again, in the court of Pharaoh

Amun! 'O Pharaoh, in this difficult situation, it could be a great relief to you if you can find the *Book of the Dead*, maybe, it will make your problem easy or help you. So, why don't you try to get this book as soon as possible? First, you must earn that solid geometric device of solid gold from the palace of Seti which you mentioned earlier.'

Pharaoh, Haman, and Amun arriving at Seti's palace, look closely at the scripts and various paintings on the walls of the palace. Pharaoh looks at a picture on which a device of that solid geometric shape is made. When Ramesses pushes a picture, a mechanical process starts and some small drawer starts opening back and forth.

After a complex mechanical process, a small cube starts coming out and opening marvelously. In it, that solid hexagonal shape of the golden device becomes visible.

Pharaoh put up the golden hexagonal device by raising his hand. The device was radiating some spectacle rays even in Pharaoh's hand.

Haman and Amun were very happy to see that solid golden shape. Pharaoh shows that shape to Amun. Amun creates finger pressure on a particular point at a solid shape in a shivering hand, instantly from the solid shape, some pointed parts open up outwards.

Amun makes the pressure of the fingers by rotating the

figure slightly, then the shape opens up from the top and takes the form of a salver, seeing with a focus on a salver, the pictured map becomes visible to reach the *Book of the Dead.*

Amun then shows the open map to Ramesses. Ramesses takes the map in his hand and looks closely. It is a map of Queen Hatshepsut's temple, based on thousands of pillars, and was very well understood by Pharaoh Ramesses.

The map had shown a golden door with a female mark for solid geometry objects. There was a straight path ahead of which many pictures were drawn on both sides. In front, the sun illuminated a book placed on a high base; in this way, this map was giving a complete view of the existence of the *Book of the Dead.*

Amun tells Pharaoh! 'O great Pharaoh! Great Seti and earlier Pharaoh have been keeping all their divine powers in this temple of Queen Hatshepsut. Apart from this, all the royal treasures of the deity God Ra and deity God Horus in these temples are also protected by the same divine powers.

'It will be impossible for centuries for anyone to reach up to these Miraculous Powers without the blessing of the sky Gods and this hexagonal divine key due to the curse of Queen Hatshepsut. But a head of state followed by the heir-apparent or one of the kings offspring born into his branch could retain them.'

Haman! 'O great Pharaoh! You are the one fully entitled to the retention of such divine powers. We have also succeeded in getting this marvelous divine key.'

In this way, Pharaoh, Haman, and Amun reach outside the temple of Queen Hatshepsut. The temple of Queen Hatshepsut was designed by Senenmut, the temple had three levels and the three of them reflect an accurately featured colonnade. The temple featured a large stone ramp from the first courtyard to the second level. Walking through the first courtyard (ground level), one could go directly through the archways on either side (which led down alleys to small ramps up to the second level) or stroll up the central ramp whose entrance was flanked by statues of lions. On the second level, there were two reflecting pools and Hor-e-Akhet lining the pathway to another ramp which brought up to the third level.

Going inside the temple, according to the map, by opening a number of doors they reached a particular door. According to the map, Pharaoh, Haman, and Amun arrived at the chamber of the courtyard of Queen Hatshepsut which was pictured on the map. Signs of all the great deities were made on this door and there was a place for putting the divine key in the middle. Pharaoh put the device over the place and turned it to the right, the door started to open with a very loud voice, and the way to the path became visible.

Amun said, 'O our great Pharaoh! Proceeding beyond this supernatural entrance from here is forbidden for us, according to royal charters, and due to the curse of Queen Hatshepsut. Therefore, we are not willing to go further, but you should go ahead and bring that divine book.'

Pharaoh! 'O Haman and Amun! Since both of you are my trustee and faithful vizier, and I have full faith in you too, then both of you should follow me, so that we can see the Holy Book with our eyes.'

Amun with terribly fear! 'O Pharaoh! None can go even a step further from here due to the curse of Queen Hatshepsut unless he has this divine key in their hand, and whoever enters the basements of this temple without that divine instrument will be cursed. That is why we are unable to go ahead, you should go ahead and bring back that Holy Book.'

Then Pharaoh entered inside alone, and soon this mysterious entrance started closing again. When that door was completely closed, the inside became dark and nothing was visible.

Pharaoh opened out the mysterious golden key in his hand, it opened in a floral shape, and a blue light scattered out of it and spread all around.

As soon as the rays scattered about the inner chamber of the palace from this divine key, some action started taking place inside the palace and many pillars of white light became visible.

When these pillars in the inner chamber were shining with divine white light, and the entire basement was also filled with divine light, there were heaps of gold figurines and diamonds and jewels all around in this chamber.

Pharaoh moved ahead through these gold and pearl embosses, as depicted on the map, he saw a golden chest in front of him. Treasures were scattered all over there.

Now Pharaoh placed the golden divine key in a designated place on the chest. The Golden Hex key itself starts rotating on its axis, as it starts rotating, its chest also starts opening slightly, and dense blue divine light is scattered all around from the chest.

The *Book of the Dead* becomes visible in the inner chest with amazing electric rays all around.

As Pharaoh raises his hands toward the book, it comes up amazingly. Pharaoh picks up the book in his hands and walks outward.

On the outer side of the courtyard of Queen Hatshepsut's temple, Pharaoh shows that book to Haman and Amun.

Amun (in a state of great glory)! 'O great Pharaoh! Whoever possesses this divine *Book of the Dead*, on earth, no one will be able to kill him by deceit or fraud. A dead person can be restored with the help of this book according to the deity of God Ra who will have this divine key.'

Haman (with a lot of air)! 'O great Pharaoh! As you have acquired this deity of God Ra, you should not be afraid of anything. In your great kingdom of Egypt, all the stayers must bow in front of the great Pharaoh. No unseen Lord would be worshiped in Egypt. The great Pharaoh will be the only God in Egypt.'

Both Haman and Amun bowed their heads in front of Pharaoh there and orders from the royal court of Egypt were released to bow their head in front of the scriptures of the great Pharaoh and consider Pharaoh to be their biggest God.

Big representations were raised in large numbers and issued orders to bow themselves before them. In Egypt, strict prohibition was imposed on the worship of any God other than Ramesses. Who did not do so, would be faced with terrible punishment. When Bani Israel refused to obey this command, Vizier Haman darted Bani Israel into the collective construction projects of giant palaces, temples, and slanted pyramids, from the orders of the royal palace.

Queen Isetnofret

Lord of Oracle – Amen-Nakht

One day while all the Futurists and predictors were eyeing in the sky, a star in the dawn emerged in the sky for which they were restless. When this star appeared, the sky was illuminated by a bright divine light. Seeing that bright star, noise erupted in the field, and at the same time, in Bani Israel's camp also, noise erupted on seeing this star. They had been waiting for this sign for years. Now they saw the situation, and all the Futurists and astrologers ran towards the Pharaoh's palace.

In the presence of Pharaoh, Haman, Amun, and other courtiers.

Amen-Nakht (little afraid)! 'O great Pharaoh! Today we have seen the sign which you have been waiting for, and it is a dare for you, after forty days from now, that the spirit will be transformed into the stomach of his mother from their father's side.'

Hearing the news, Pharaoh and Haman became somewhat restless.

Haman cunningly! 'O our companion Amen-Nakht! If you give us this prediction, you can also tell us from your vision who is the mother of that upcoming spirit, and who is the father; that way should make it a little easier.'

Pharaoh inclined and paid attention to Amen-Nakht. Amen-Nakht said, 'O Haman! The owner of our livelihood… as much as our vision tells us, we have told you, nothing more we have to tell.'

Hearing this debate Pharaoh and Haman both got very angry

over Amen-Nakht.

In the meantime, Amun came forward a bit.

Amun said, 'O great Pharaoh! Our companion, Amen-Nakht, said right now, just after forty days that the spirit is transforming in his mother's stomach. Is this not enough for us to think something? What else do we need?'

Everybody was very impressed by this illustration. The old Amen-Nakht and the accompanying disciples also felt some relief, which had come to the fore just a little earlier due to the anger of the Pharaoh.

Amun referring toward Amen-Nakht, 'Thank you very much, our respected companion… Now go to the palace happily and enjoy the blessings and hospitality of the great Pharaoh.'

Old Amen-Nakht and his disciples, in this way, leave the court of Pharaoh.

Amun, 'O great Pharaoh! Those very experienced provident magicians have made your difficulty a little easier. You should show your mercy to them. Now, if you have to do something about what has already been revealed that night on which that spirit will transform in his mother's stomach, then that night we should manage in such a way that every man of Egypt must spend the whole night in the forest with his all-male children. Only women will stay in their homes. King Ahmose's celestial Army should be put on the doors of Egypt. No one should be allowed to enter the city, and this work should be done with great stealth.'

Haman and all the royal courtiers present there appreciated it.

In this way, the order was issued that from today on the fortieth night, all the male residents of Egypt would spend the night in the forest with the great Pharaoh. All the male and male children of Egypt would join in the celebration. This was a royal order, and everyone was bound by this.

Bani Israel also ordered the same that every man of the community spend his nights in the forest with his adult and minor males and celebrate the compassion of the great Pharaoh.

Again, on time, Pharaoh, Haman, courtiers, all the viziers along with Egyptians and Bani Israel gathered at the outer deep forest.

The entire wilderness forest was buzzing today. All the Egyptians and Bani Israel were also soon engulfed in the game and the pageant. There was a wide variety of food and drink at the royal cuisine.

The tablecloth was spread long on the ground, full of delicious dishes and fruits. Bani Israel was soon involved in a very well-received and heavily enjoyed tribute.

Amun and Haman, summoned all the predictors and magicians and instructed them, 'All of you stay alert all night, keep an eye on the sky, and beware that there is not too much gossip for even a moment!'

Predictors and magicians have focused now their eyes on the sky. On the other hand, more than half of these most oblivious Egyptian men and children went to play and eat. Pharaoh was also constantly eyeing this scene from his camp. When the last portion of the night begins, the Pharaoh calls his vizier Haman and says, 'Haman! Now it is going to be daybreak, so I go to the palace. You keep looking at the situation here.'

Pharaoh to their vizier Amran, 'O Amran! You are my bonafide vizier, so you go to the palace with us.'

Thus, vizier Amran, who was the vizier and looked after and guarded the palaces of Pharaoh, took the great Pharaoh in a chariot and departed toward the palace. They both entered the palace there, exhausted; Pharaoh entered his palace.

Vizier Amran appointed himself at the palace gate in a safe and alert mode.

On the other hand, some women of Bani Israel have gone out in the night to see the palace of Pharaoh, they also have vizier Amran's wife. When all the women pass before the palace of the Pharaoh, Amran's eyes are on them. They all move forward looking at the palace with high and luxurious plains. When Amran's beautiful wife sees the vizier Amran who was posted at the grand entrance there, her feet become a little slower instantaneously.

Other side, the women of Bani Israel crossed ahead, seeing the huge statues built outside Pharaoh's Palaces. Amran keeps his wife with him and in the palace alone where they both meet each other. And in the last of daybreak, when the holy spirit transformed into their mother's stomach as mentioned in the religious book, immediately a star becomes visible in the sky. The land of Egypt lights up from this star shining. As if every star in the sky is illuminating many times more than its original intensity. And that prophet's star splashes together on a very heavy light ground. Every grass straw of that dense forest became illuminated to welcome the holy spirit.

On the side, Bani Israel was staying, a person of Bani Israel saw it first; he happily made the other people of the community aware of this and said, 'O my community! Congratulations to you... It is the same sign that you waited for so many years.' Very rarely will you get rid of the junky slavery. On the other hand, Futurists and astrologers started making huge noises in the field when they saw these signs in the sky. Bani Israelis were also making noise in happiness.

In this way, there was a huge noise erupting on the ground. Futurists and predictors were blushing dust in the air, expressing raving. The uproar of this huge noise erupted so much that it reached the palaces of Pharaoh. He got up in fear and looked out from the high terrace of his palace. Seeing Amran down there, he asked, 'O Amran! How is this noise in the forest there?'

Amran! 'I believe that they are in uproar from the joy of the kindness great Pharaoh makes over them; they are playing and in the spectacle of sports.'

Hearing this, Pharaoh returned, but the relief to Pharaoh was flown. When it was morning, all predictors and astrologers gathered outside the palace with dust minted over the head. Appearing in front of Pharaoh, they expressed, 'Awesome, Pharaoh! The first half of the night passed very well, but on the day before, we saw thousands of snipers and symbols in the sky in front of our eyes. We warn you in our belief that the spirit has transformed in the dawn to his mother's stomach from their father's side.'

On hearing the news, Pharaoh and his courtiers became highly disappointed.

Haman! 'O our trustworthy brother, can you tell us from your knowledge of the book who is the mother of that holy spirit, and who the father is?'

Predictors turn pale in fear. 'O our master! we have told you, as much as we have been able to know from our knowledge, and we know no more.'

Hearing this from predictors, Pharaoh became very frightening.

Pharaoh! 'Child is born in Bani Israel from today, if a boy is born, then he should be killed immediately, and if a girl is born then she should be left alive.'

Hearing this uproar, all the courtiers and predictors got shocked and very upset.

And in this way, thousands of children of Bani Israel were slaughtered at the hands of Pharaoh. While the sons of Bani Israel were being murdered in the procession of Pharaoh for years. One day, an Egyptian came to the court of Pharaoh and said, 'O great Pharaoh! If the children of Bani Israel continue to be slaughtered in the same way, then from where will we get slaves to get our help and where will we get labor-power as slaves for the construction projects of your city, Ramesses? So, it is our request to you to stop this murder process!'

After the advice from the courtiers, Haman issues the order.

'O Egyptians! After listening to all your pleas, it is ordered by Pharaoh from today that the male children born one year will be allowed to live and the male children born next year will be killed.'

So, in this way, Moses' brother Aaron was born in a year in which there was no order to kill.

Moses' Birth

While Amran's wife got pregnant, no sign was revealed of pregnancy and no one was informed about this gesture and no midwife was even deputed.

In this way, when the time came for the child to be born and Amran's wife felt child pain, only the woman and a daughter were present in the house.

When it is time for the merciful to descend, then a light, like a moon, shone down. So, in a hurry, the holy soul was born quickly.

The mother feeds the delighted holy soul soon so that no sound is left outside the house. She even kept this child from his relatives and neighbors for many days. She remained busy for a few days in care with a loving beautiful face.

But that mother used to think every time that if the voice of this child got outside the house and then Pharaoh was informed about it, then the soldiers of Pharaoh would take this child and kill him.

So, after a few days of feeding her beloved son, she arranged to get a wooden box from a woodworker. One day, after putting a soft cloth in it, she laid down her beloved son and after closing the chest, both mother and daughter took him to the River Nile

After reaching there and opening the box one more time, the mother finds that the child is very comfortable lying in it.

Mother put a stone on the heart, closed the box, and before anyone saw it, she dumped the box in the River (Darya-e-Neel) Nile. In this way, both of them turned toward the house shedding tears, and the mother's heart became desperate.

The mother told the daughter that she should hide and keep an eye on the receptacle floating in the river and see what the result was. In this way, the receptacle flowed through the drainage.

The little girl was keeping an eye on the chest from the clump of reeds on the banks of the river Darya-e-Neel. The chest was moving forward floating on the waves of Darya-e-Neel, and that little girl was hiding in front and continued chasing that chest. The chest was moving along the waves in an equally long, wide Darya-e-Neel.

There, on the banks of Darya-e-Neel, which was the place where Pharaoh's royal ladies took their bath, the women of Pharaoh came to the bank of Darya-e-Neel. This part of the palace was reserved for only the royal ladies to take baths and bathe in the Nile. Queen Isetnofret reached there and left all her clothes, golden straps, neck collars, except a few underclothes, and started swimming in the waves of Darya-e-Neel.

Queen Isetnofret was adept at swimming, so she floated far ahead in the Nile River. The maids who came with Queen Isetnofret were looking at Darya-e-Neel standing in the palace on the banks and muttering in jest. When the queen came far ahead while swimming, it was seen that a wooden chest was riding on its side. And the sound of the baby crying was coming out of it.

So, seeing this scene, Queen Isetnofret brought the box to the floating shore, and she lifted the box from the water with her own hands. Despite that she was wearing only her short bathing clothes at that time, the child's cry made Isetnofret forget everything else.

When taken from the river, it was not a surprise when she opened the box. A very beautiful child lay crying in the chest.

Seeing this scene, Queen Isetnofret woke up and the love of that child was born in her heart.

Queen Isetnofret lifted the child and started kissing its face like the moon. So, the child fell silent on attaching by Queen Isetnofret to her chest. The love of the child replaced her heart. On the other hand, this child's sister was watching this scene from the distance between the clumps of trees in the River Nile.

Queen Isetnofret took this child to the palace. Hearing this story, Pharaoh came to the palace to see the child.

Pharaoh said, 'O Isetnofret! Where did you find this beautiful face?'

Queen Isetnofret! 'This child is the apple of mine and your eyes. Do not kill it. Why don't we make it our son? I think that this benefits us.'

Pharaoh said (in the lap of Moses), 'O Isetnofret! I don't need this, but you have permission to make him your son.'

Of course, here Pharaoh, Haman, and his Army had missed...!

Now Queen Isetnofret is happily engaged in the care of her child. Queen Isetnofret called the midwives to feed the child, but the child did not even mouth any milk.

On the other hand, this little girl tells her mother that the ark reaches the palace of the Pharaoh and is taken out by the women of the palace. Upon hearing this, Mother's heart became desperate, but she strengthened her heart that the mother's love should not be opened so that the child's condition was known to everyone. So, she stayed in the house to firmly stop her heart aching.

On the other hand, thousands of women were coming to the royal palace to offer themselves to feed the sons of the Pharaoh, but the child would not touch any milk. In the same way, when many days passed, it was made known in the city that a woman was needed to feed the son of the Pharaoh.

Pharaoh would open the doors of mercy on her and show favor. So, at one place, that little girl told the courtiers that she should tell them the way to a house where she could feed this child and raise her well and be treated with love. In this way, the girl came running to the house and told her mother that in the palace of Pharaoh, her son had not drunk any woman's milk for many days. And they want a woman to feed the Pharaoh's son in his palace. That way the mother of the child was brought to the palace with great care. At that time, Pharaoh was also present. When put in the lap of a covered woman, he immediately started drinking milk.

Seeing this, Pharaoh was surprised. She was not the real mother of this child. The mother of the child replied wisely with her face covered, because this child was the great son of Pharaoh, and he hardly liked the milk of the common woman. But I am a docile woman, and my milk is very clean and sheer; it is just that your son likes to drink my milk. Apart from this, your son, if you bring any other child to me, then he too will start drinking my milk happily. This way, Pharaoh understood this.

Pharaoh (being happy) said, 'Go, from today onwards, feed this child with a lot of grit carry him to your house, and bring him up well.

'We will spare you and make you happy. And bring it to the royal palace once a week to cool Isetnofret's eyes with it.'

And thus that child got a place in the palace of Pharaoh. This also made Queen Isetnofret very happy, and the few women present there congratulated the son of Queen Isetnofret.

Queen Isetnofret now took this son in her lap. Then a woman said, 'You are blessed with your lovely son, but you should also name it something.'

'I should. Because I have extracted him from water and the River Nile, so he should be named Moses.' And then everyone congratulated Queen Isetnofret. All of them loved and praised Moses very much, and thus Moses was raised as a son of Pharaoh in the palace.

Queen Isetnofret was unashamedly in love with Moses. After some time, when Moses grew up a little, one day in the full court of Pharaoh, Haman, Amun, and all the courtiers were discussing the situation at some point.

And Moses sat in the lap of Pharaoh. Queen Isetnofret was also sitting on the throne of the queen at the same time.

There was a royal necklace of gold and jewels on the neck of the Pharaoh, Moses struck it with a strong hand; the necklace broke down from the neck of Pharaoh and went down to the ground and its pearls were going to break away on the ground.

Pharaoh, Haman, Queen Isetnofret, Amun, and all the courtiers were surprised by this act of the child.

There was silence all over the court. Such a small child twisted such a strong necklace and threw it on the ground.

Pharaoh fearing the zeal of the child Moses, got harsh and gave a stern command! 'Haman, Take this child from here and slaughter it immediately.'

On this, the Queen Isetnofret came in the middle.

Queen Isetnofret said, 'O great Pharaoh! Don't do this, because children often do this and the glowing pearls near them and the embers of the burning fire are equal. It is still small, and its antics are not weighed in the scale of wisdom.'

Vizier Haman cautiously and cleverly revolved around the eyes. 'Queen Isetnofret! Well, let us test it.' At the same time, shining pearls and jewels and red embers of the burning fire were summoned in a pan. And after Moses was seated on the ground, both of them were placed before Moses.

Queen Isetnofret became very restless. Haman and all the courtiers were looking at this with astonished eyes. At first, Moses put a pearl and jewels on his knee, and Isetnofret's heartbeat stopped.

But then the child turned toward the embers of the blazing fire and picked up one ember by hand and put it in his mouth immediately.

Due to which the tongue of Moses got burnt a bit, and in the future, a new look was born in his tongue.

At that point, Isetnofret descended from the throne and took the beloved Moses in her arms, and the anger of Pharaoh was relieved. And Moses' upbringing and tactics continued in the palace of Pharaoh.

Then after a few days—

Every day in the palace of Pharaoh, there was a permanent arrangement of communion dinner for a long time, millions of people were eating food at this level for a long time. The palace used to have a long and long queue on which any rich and poor could eat food.

One day, the royal tablecloth was installed. Along with the Pharaoh, Queen Isetnofret and the royal family also attended the traditional food space. On the outside, there was a decorum for all the courtiers and there was an opportunity for everyone in this along with the royal family.

Moses also came to the tablecloth to eat along with the royal family. Incidentally, a full roasted lamb was kept in a tray on the tablecloth in front of Moses. So, Moses stared at the stronghold immediately, and there were lots of anger expressions emerging from Moses' face with sweating.

Everyone was horrified to see such a condition of Moses. Nobody could start eating. Even the Pharaoh was not understanding anything. In such a situation, Moses pointed with an index finger toward the roasted lamb and said, 'Go, stand up!' Then the sky above the palace struck a flash of lightning that shook the hearts of the every people present there.

So, the roasted lamb stood upright and started making the voice of 'Mey-Mey' by looking around, everyone's face present there, turned yellow upon seeing this amazing feat.

Pharaoh himself was scared, there on the tablecloth without eating anything, everyone's senses flew away. The Pharaoh was looking at Queen Isetnofret with his open mouth.

There were no words to say. Pharaoh could not understand anything. Just then, Queen Isetnofret called Moses and hid Moses in her arms, and turned toward Pharaoh.

'O great Pharaoh! This thing is the plea of your great son to be very promising and becoming great. Moses will rule in your great empire. And your fame will be common in all the world, and it will carry forward the great legacy of your great empire of Egypt.'

Pharaoh had nothing but surprise. Haman, in such a time, used to give some vomit-direct advice to Pharaoh, but at this time his wit had also flown away. He was not yet in a condition to open his mouth in this situation.

Now the Queen Isetnofret indicated that everyone should start eating at the royal tablecloth. And in between the circumstances, and in the strange situations, the upbringing of Moses continued in the palace of Pharaoh under the care of Queen Isetnofret.

And Moses reached his youth.

When Moses came out of the city wearing a nice dress and

riding in a chariot, people thought that Moses was the son of a Pharaoh and a soft-hearted princess.

Once, when Moses came out of the city on a royal ride, he took the approach to Ramesses city through the valley of temples. Passing through the huge statues and temples, passing through the front of the huge statue of Hor-e-Akhet, and approaching the three big pyramids of Emperor Khefran.

Moses was not interested in these large statues and huge buildings. So, Moses went ahead in view of these grand creations. Here, millions of slaves were working hard day and night on the huge collective construction project.

It was a city called Ramesses, being built on the orders of Pharaoh who used to work on a lot of construction projects by giants and slaves in very strict and fraudulent ways. Millions of slaves wearing only the loincloth (Schenti) of white linen clothing that was common to all the slaves with the rest of the body naked were executed on temples and other projects in typical situations under the demons engaged in construction project.

Pharaoh had long ago decreed the order to Egyptians as well as Bani Israel. "Because I provide you eatables; I am the one who nurses you; so my confession rests on you all. I am only your greatest God. Egyptians obeyed this command of the Pharaoh, but Bani Israel refused to accept it."

So, Pharaoh commanded Bani Israel that if you do not accept me as your God and you will accept someone other, then I will complicate you in great pain and trouble.

Young Bani Israelis were deputed in the work of cutting stones. He ordered the old and the weak to work hard all day and submit their earnings to the royal treasury before sunset. The pregnant women of Bani Israel also used to carry stones. Bani

Israel does not fit himself in the environment in the hands of giants nor the way to escape.

Demons had call upon the earth to lift the massive stones using the power of wind and some supernatural frequencies. They also created a powerful field of force and vibrations around a construction project that enabled them to roll away the massive stone cubes upward to build the construction. When Moses passed by the people, he saw that the behavior of big giants was highly crucial to the people of Bani Israel.

The giants and demons were beating these slaves like animals and getting them to do the most difficult tasks. Moses noticed at one place that a slave woman was offering water to a weak laborer slave who was wrapped in all the soil.

A woman was trying to drink water from her water pot when an oppressive demon hit her with a whip, resulting innocent woman of Bani Israel with the water pot falling on one side.

Demon whipped the slave worker and started stripping his skin from the body.

Moses jumped from his chariot seeing this oppression and snatched his whip from the bloodthirsty demon and picked up that water vessel and gave water to the slave.

Demons were frightened to find this son of the Pharaoh here and immediately fell in front of Moses. Moses did not pay attention to him and watered that slave with one hand on his mouth that was covered with mud.

When this whole thing happened, the community of Bani Israel in a strange situation saw that the son of Pharaoh was offering water with his hand to a slave, seeing this they were surprised a lot.

They just kept watching this view with their dry expectant eyes.

Now when Moses moved on from here, every Bani Israel seeing this Messiah, felt the coolness of cold water in his heart and was watching toward Moses with hope.

Moses proceeded from there with his chariot and went to another construction project where the construction work of a pyramid was going on.

The design of tetrahedron pyramids was based on scared geometry having spiritual significance and harmony with the natural world and shape intended to harness spiritual energy. Shape and orientation were carefully calculated to align with certain celestial energies and divine forces. The shape of the pyramid was a symbol, or sun rays that were the source of all life and giving energy to the mummies restored and help them in their journey to after life. Heavy stones were being drawn on which various pictures were made by hieroglyphs. The cubical stones were very heavy, and they were being pulled by manipulating the elements of nature. They possess incredible powers that allowed them to control gravity, earth, water, air, and fire. They used spiritual practice and certain frequencies that enabled them to move massive stones to build the structure.

In addition to thousands of demons pulling stones up the slope using certain frequencies, and understanding the basic concepts of gravity, two rails were made on the slope on which those heavy stones would move a little easier. There were such mechanical arms in the middle of the two tracks, in such a way that the heavy stone could move forward but could not move back and forth.

In addition to the heavily painted stones moving up on these slopes, demons, and slaves were engaged on the ground to pull many more stones. In this way, Moses was standing there watching how these slaves were captivated by this heavy struggle.

Moses noticed that one of the aged slaves who was in a row to pull a heavy stone fell between two tracks due to the heavy strength of thirst. Other slaves were pulling stones without any notice, who had fallen from them, and who was still standing.

The aged slave was lying between two tracks and that heavy pyramid stone was moving fast toward him. As soon as the huge block had just arrived to grind the aged slave, the slaves who were pulling the huge stone, got shocked.

The stone stopped. Despite all of them putting in a lot of effort, they were not able to move even a bit of the heavy block.

The demon inflicted whips on the slaves, but the stone did not move from its place, despite exerting full effort! When the demon's eyes went to the stone, he found Moses alone standing there holding the heavy stone with both his hands.

And the fallen slave was lying in the middle of Moses' feet. When the demon saw Moses there, he immediately fell prostrate.

When the slaves also turned back, they found a man holding the stone.

Moses ordered the slaves to stop the work and arranged water for the fallen slave. When all this was done, then another artisan of the place came there because the work of moving all the blocks behind had stopped.

Then Moses ordered the artisan and cyclopes present there to provide water to the entire group of slaves engaged in construction projects and to stop all the work for a while.

Then Moses proceeded from there, he reached a place where a thousand slaves were engaged in erecting a large heavy sculpture of Pharaoh made of a solid stone and lying on the tracks.

That sculpture of solid stone was some three hundred cubits

long and fifty cubits wide. At the bottom of this sculpture, different types of pictures were written in hieroglyphs, and in hieroglyphs, many ruling countries of Pharaoh were written.

The sculpture of solid stone was so big that Moses was able to reach its last tip only after walking for a long time. Moses saw that thousands of slaves were imprisoned in many places by iron threads with thick ropes.

Most of the ropes on the top side of the sculpture were tied in strong threads of iron, while the other end of the rope was tied with heavy-weighing stones. Some of the heavy iron girdles attached to the sculpture were moving inside heavy iron-heavy hexagonal mechanical devices attached to the chains.

These chains of iron were being pulled in and out through the many roars moving inside these mechanical devices so that the heavy sculpture was lifting from one side.

Thousands of slaves held the ropes on both sides. On the other hand, even thousands of slaves were able to erect this sculpture directly through ropes. Moses saw that behind this heavy sculpture, four similar were being dragged by thousands of slaves to be brought to the same site.

Moses saw that this task of erecting the sculpture upright was being conducted from a particular place nearby. Moses leaves his chariot there and reaches the place to operate the project. When Moses arrives at that place, all the people, including the chief artisan, Ankhenamesh, who is involved in the project, are shocked and bow down before Moses.

Moses, ignoring them, sees that the huge statue of the great Pharaoh is half-erect at a particular angle.

Here also hungry-thirsty slaves are engaged in handling the huge sculpture of Pharaoh. In addition to these countless slaves, some complex mechanical devices were also assigned to work in this complex process.

There was a constant threat to those slaves on the other side that this sky-high sculpture of Pharaoh holding the crown of Upper Egypt and Lower Egypt on his head with Nemesh may cush over them.

Finally, Ankhenamesh felt a little relief when this huge statue of Pharaoh stood upright in his place. Then he turned his attention to Moses. Moses said to Ankhenamesh, 'O Ankhenamesh! In these huge construction projects, in which these slaves suffer day and night and they work so hard, are they forbidden to drink water, even when you see many slaves are thirsty without water? Whereas, I see that millions of people eat food every day on the tablecloth of great Pharaoh. Then why this awful treatment over this poor community when even they are longing for water, even though, they work with the heaviest effort from them.'

Ankhenamesh! 'You see that we do all the work here under royal orders. Here all the projects are controlled under the orders of Vizier Haman. You can issue whatever you want. We see that you are a noble and justice-loving prince, so why do you not dictate your command?'

Moses! 'I order you now that the community of all these slaves should be provided water, and the seventh day of the week should be a day of rest. So, no work should be taken from any slave on that day.'

Hearing these orders, all the demons present there were upset and began to mourn.

Then Moses went among Bani Israel and blessed them and consecrated the seventh day of the week among them holy, that is to say, that day was a day of rest for all works. It was held as a day of rest.

Thus, when this matter reached the court of the Pharaohs, Moses was ordered to attend the court.

In the Court of Pharaoh

A demon said, 'O great Pharaoh! Your son Moses has great kindness over you slaves, those who are engaged in the construction project on your city of Ramesses. Moses has even obstructed the work of royal construction sites there, and he has a strong sympathy over those who refuse your Lordship. And we fully doubt that Moses himself is also denying you as his God.

Pharaoh (turning from Moses) 'O dear Moses! What is your recognition of me being a God...? Who is your God?'

Moses answered! 'My God is the one who feeds me, and the one who has made me grow up.'

Pharaoh happily 'Moses! You told the truth. In reality, I am the one who feeds you, and I am the one who has made you grow bigger, and those who make a lie about you, are liars. Go and no harm to you.'

So, Moses withdrew from there.

Moses often used to go among the people of the Bani Israel, the poor community that was involved in hard work, weakened.

Pharaoh had long slaughtered the boys of Bani Israel and allowed the girls to live. Moses was always inconsolable at seeing this gimmick of Pharaoh.

In order to reduce this sorrow, Moses often went among the Bani Israel to help them. Bani Israelis used to tell this noble-hearted prince about their suffering; and how Pharaoh had weakened his community. Takes hard work from our men, and makes our elders and pregnant women carry stones. Bani Israel is in great trouble.

And with the hope from our elders, about a prophecy that someone will come who will relieve us from this great trouble, we have been waiting for that spirit for years.

Moses with Prophet Sueb

The treatment of the Egyptians was very painful and slanderous toward the people of Bani Israel, seeing this Moses's heart had remained always inconsolable.

Moses often used to go among these people to see the pain and grief of their lives. Bani Israelis also came to sit in love with this soft-hearted prince and began to speak with Moses of their sufferings that were imposed over their community by Pharaoh and Haman.

People said, 'O Moses! Pharaoh has been oppressing us since before your birth, and this oppression of Egyptians continues to grow on us to this day. Now see when we get redemption from this oppression.'

Moses consults them, 'What you ask from your Lord? He is not strange, he will spare you a lot and frees you from Pharaoh's grip, and may make you the owner of this city.'

So, one day, Moses passed by the market where people were in their homes due to the heavy heat outside. On this way, he saw two people quarreling with each other. Coming nearby, Moses saw a man from the castle of the Pharaoh beating a poor slave of Bani Israel with a whip.

Upon finding Moses present there, the man of Bani Israel shouted to get help from Moses. 'Hey, Moses, help me in this matter.'

Moses was already angry. He proceeded to settle the matter and, to settle the quarrel, punch the face of an Egyptian man who was the man from the palace of the Pharaoh. With a punch, the man from the castle of the Pharaoh collapsed and died as soon as he fell to the ground.

Seeing this circumstance, that person of Bani Israel ran away from there. Moses saw here and there that no one saw him doing this and went away from there and no one was informed of this murder.

Now Moses felt very sad and thought in his heart that this work was of Satan, then raised his hands and said, 'O Owner of land and sky! If I persecute myself, will you forgive on my crime as you are the one who sees everything and you are very forgiving?'

On the second day when Moses passed through there to check the situation, he saw that the man of Bani Israel who had sought help from Moses yesterday was fighting with another Egyptian man. Seeing Moses there, he asked for help again. In response Moses said to that person of Bani Israel with a strong tone – 'You are a very bad man that you have to fight with someone every day.'

And intending to end the quarrel, Moses pulled the man of Bani Israel aside with strong hands, and then the man of Bani Israel shouted, 'O Moses! Have you become infatuated with murder? Like the way you slaughtered the man yesterday, you wish to kill me in the same way!'

Listening to these words, the Egyptian man immediately ran toward the court of Pharaoh, shouting.

On reaching Pharaoh's court, the Egyptian said that yesterday the man of your kitchen, who was murdered and whose murderer is being searched all over Egypt, his murderer is Moses, and we are the witnesses.

On hearing this message from this man, Pharaoh became very disappointed and consulted their courtiers about the circumstances.

Haman gave a thought in the ears of the Pharaoh.

Haman! 'I was sure from the very first day that this boy is definitely the one who will destroy you and your country one day! So, now a good chance of his murder has come out in your hand because Moses has killed the man of your royal palace. In whose vengeance, the order to kill Moses should be issued immediately.'

Pharaoh was very weak from their ear's side.

He immediately issued the order, 'Moses should be present in the court tomorrow, and tomorrow, he will be sentenced to death for the murder of the royal man.'

At the same time, there were many such men in the court of Pharaoh who were well-versed in the personality of Moses and considered Moses to be their companion.

So, one of those men came running from the tip of the city and said to the beloved Moses, 'O Moses! Have you some information that plans are being made for your murder? If you have to do something then do it, so that you get out quickly from Egypt or else you will be killed.'

Hearing these things, Moses immediately went out of the city through the big buildings and idols of Egypt in the night and took the path of the east in the deep forest.

The next day when the sun rose, Moses was out of the city of Egypt. From there, only some high Egyptian sculptures and pyramids were visible.

A little to the right was the city of Ramesses where work was underway on several construction projects that had not yet been completed which were visible from there.

Moses continued his journey day and night, even in the scorching heat in the deep forest. And thus, after seven days and seven nights continuously walking toward the east direction, Moses reached the forest of Madaian, hungry and thirsty. Moses walked and drifted through the dust-balloon.

Hungry and thirsty, he sat there under a tree to rest a little. After a while, he saw that some shepherds had reached there with their goats, and they pushed a heavy stone to one side which was on a clean water well. Then together, everyone drew a big pot of water with great force and poured out the water which filled in a pit made of long mud.

So, the goats of those shepherds started drinking water. Moses saw the two shy girls standing at some distance, who were standing there stopping their goats.

Moses was watching all these views sitting under the tree there. So, those shepherds watered their goats and all of them joined the heavy stone again and covered it in the well. And did not take any care of the goats of those shy girls and took their way.

Now both of them brought their goats forward and whatever was the leftover water, the girl's goats started licking it.

Seeing this, Moses felt mercy, he came toward the girls and asked, 'Who are you?'

One of the girls blushing, 'Our father is old and does not even see by eye. We have to do all the household work. The water that is left from the goats of these people, we give to our goats and return to home.'

Moses was shocked after hearing about this incident.

Though Moses was hungry and thirsty for the last many days and was exhausted from the journey, he came to a state of anger.

He single-handedly threw the heavy stone on the well's mouth to one side. And the pot, which was pulled by five or six men together, was pulled out and poured out, and gave them plenty of water for the goats of both shy girls.

And when the goats had drunk a lot of water, both of them went to their house offering prayers to Moses. And Moses returned to the shadow of that tree and turned his face to the sky. Speaking, 'God! I am enchanted by your kindness. Whatever good thing you bring to me, I am in need of it.'

The two shy girls, whose goats Moses had given the water to, were the companions of Prophet Sueb, whose father had become blind in his old age.

Like every day when the two girls reached home with their goats, their blind father habitually saw the goats on their stomachs, today, he felt that the goats were more out of their way, then he happily asked both girls about today's circumstances. Both the girls communicated the sympathy and good faith of that kind-hearted traveler and also told that when they turned to the house, the traveler sat in the shadow of a tree and turned his face toward the sky, he asked, 'God! I am enchanted by your kindness. Whatever good thing you bring to me, I need it.'

On hearing this communication, the whole glory of Sueb's inner soul came to know, then he said, 'Sadly, the traveler is in a state of trouble and is in a state of hunger, and he is asking for bread from his God. So, my daughter, you go early and bring him home and feed him. I know that he has not eaten anything for the last seven days. So, my daughter, you go and bring him home. I doubt that food will be left in this city from God, for not giving food to a traveler.'

Then a daughter of Prophet Sueb left to take the traveler home.

And when she reached there, she saw the noble traveler was still sitting in the shadow of the same tree.

The daughter of the prophet was becoming shy as she rode

up, embracing her clothes that were flying due to the wind, with her big eyes folded down and shrinking in her arm, with her high stature, shamefully blushing, she asked the noble traveler. 'Our old father is a prophet, and sends you salutations, and has called you to come to our home, that what compassion you have done on us, we pay you.'

Moses did not show any attention, but hearing the salute and the message of a prophet, immediately got up with a mind to meet them.

On ahead, that daughter of the prophet was walking with very controlled and straight steps. The strong wind was still blowing so that the girl's clothes flapped as she walked and revealed her calf.

When Moses stared at the open calf of the shy girl, he stopped and told the girl, 'I walk ahead and you follow me and take the pebbles in your hand and throw them on the side we have to go.' So, when Moses entered the house of Prophet Sueb, he saluted, and then Sueb stood up and smiled.

While making handshakes, Prophet Sueb observed some noticeable impressions on the hand of Moses, and on the face, some different emotions were revealed.

Then Sueb seated Moses with great respect and asked, 'O noble traveler! Who are you? And where did you come from?'

Moses told Prophet Sueb all the information and circumstances.

When Moses had narrated the matter, Sueb gave his consolation and said, 'God has freed you from the hold of the oppressor. Now there should be no fear of anything. Just remember that your days of hardness have gone, and you have got rid of the oppressor, now eat food leisurely and give thanks to God.'

So, the daughters served food at the same time.

The food had been kept in front of Moses, but he did not run his hands over the food.

The Prophet said after feeling! 'Merciful traveler! Why are you not eating food?'

Moses! 'I do not want to eat food in exchange for feeding your herds. This act, I did for God's sake.'

Prophet Sueb said, 'O noble traveler! This food is not just a meal from our side but is hospitality from a prophet to the guest who came to their home. I am very delighted with your noble manners and honesty. Therefore, it is a duty on you to accept my host and make my heart wrench.'

On hearing this, Moses immediately started eating food. When the two had eaten, one of Sueb's daughters, named Siphora, said to her father, Prophet Sueb, 'Abba! You can keep him as a servant here because whom you can keep as a servant owns all such qualities. They are powerful as well as insincere.'

So, Sueb asked, 'Dear daughter, what did you see in his bravery and brazenness?'

Siphora said, 'Abba! There's a well of clean water in the forest, which requires five or six men to remove the stone placed on its mouth, he removed it alone and the water pot of the well which the five-man pulled, he pulled alone and gave our goats water. And out of humiliation, he himself went ahead and told me to follow the path through stone peltings.'

Hearing this incident, Prophet Sueb turned to Moses and said, 'Farzand! I want to marry one of these two daughters to you. On the condition that you feed my goats for eight years, and if you complete ten years, it will be your favor. I do not want to put you under any strictness, and you will find me among the good people.'

Because Moses had run away from a dreadful situation to save his life, so he accepted this offer as an alumnus and honor.

Moses said, 'I appreciate your kindness, both of these issues are on me to fulfill. And in no way I will find your service difficult and you will find me firm and steady.'

On hearing this determination, Sueb was very much impressed. When Prophet Sueb handed over his goats to Moses, it was considered appropriate to give Moses a stick or Asa.

Prophet Sueb had in his custody so many of the old-fashioned prophet's sticks which had been defending him in Mirash, which were kept safely by Prophet Sueb in one of the closets of the house. There was also a twilight stick in it that breathed as if a heavy python was sleeping.

Some were such that they were shining in their light. Some were kept like this on the wall.

That closet inside Prophet Sueb's house was completely illuminated by these strange sticks. Because of their illuminations inside the cell, there was a divine light scattered all around.

Prophet Sueb said to Moses! 'Farzand! In the closet inside the house... You go there and bring one stick from there for yourself which can help you to break apart the leaves for these goats.'

The closet was illuminated in strange lights.

When Moses went to that cell, he looked closely at that cell.

There was also a small door of the closet which was carved. That small door seemed to be made of very precious metal. Moses opened the door of the metal closet and, while keeping his mouth out, put his hand inside the closet to catch any Asa (stick). The view inside the cell was something other.

Some Asa kept there were increasing their size and also

reducing themselves.

Some of them had bright light feet. Some were so red as hot iron turns red. But there was no fire. One was breathing and exhaling fiercely. When Moses extended his hand to hold a stick inside the cell, that strange Asa who was breathing and leaving breath in a terrible way, he sprang up automatically into Moses' hand. So, Moses grabbed him and took him in his hand.

When Prophet Sueb heard the sense of that strange Asa, then he recognized.

Prophet Sueb! 'Farzand, show me which stick you have brought?'

Moses handed over the stick to the hand of Prophet Sueb.

When the Prophet Sueb turned his hand on the stick, he recognized that it was just that kind of weird stick.

Then ordered, 'Farzand! Go and keep it there... bring something else.'

Moses again went to that cell and put the strange stick with reverence on one side and opened his hand for some other side to another stick, but suddenly the same stick jumped up and came into the hand of Moses. Moses brought it back to Prophet Sueb.

Prophet Sueb then turned his hand from top to bottom on the Asa (stick) and said to Moses, 'Farzand! It is not of any use to you, go, keep it there, and bring another one.'

Moses went back to the closet, he put the Asa on one side and moved his arm to the other side, and then the same Asa jumped again and came into Moses' hand.

Moses again brought the same Asa again into Sueb's hand.

On recognizing it, Prophet Sueb again said, 'Dear Farzand! You have brought the same thing again. This one is the property of someone else.

Dear Farzand! The thing is that when I got this Asa, I also

received a legacy, that this Asa should be handed over to a high-status prophet and whenever he comes into the world and it is in your responsibility to assign.'

Then Moses said, 'O my elderly! The thing is that when I keep this Asa in the closet on one side and pick up some other from the other side, then this Asa falls by itself in my hand every time.'

Prophet Sueb is shocked after hearing this. The Asa falls directly on the ground, leaving Sueb's hand, then a little more than half gets sunk into the ground.

Now Prophet Sueb tried to pull that Asa from the ground himself, but the Asa did not move from its place. Tired, Sueb turned to Moses and said, 'O Farzand! Now this Asa will be for whom, who pulls it from the ground. Now it is gone from us.'

After hearing this offer, Moses had just opened his hand toward Asa, it immediately jumped into Moses' hand. Moses with reverence gave it again into the hand of Prophet Sueb and said, 'Please, take this, here is your legacy!'

The Prophet Sueb caught it and said, 'O, dear Farzand! I understand, now it is your legacy. Never be reckless about it, because it is not an easy object. This is a strange commodity. It will work for you in every situation and will help you fully in any circumstances.'

Now Prophet Sueb was convinced that Moses was going to get some heavy responsibility in the near future. So, his heart became very happy that after so many years, the responsibility which was given to him, he had handed over safe into the righteous hands today.

Because in that closet of Prophet Sueb, there were about seventy Asa (hand stick) from the earlier high-ranking prophets, and this Asa was also there that was a very strange thing among himself. Sometimes, it used to take a shaaaa-shaaaa, breath and shout with great emphasis, which is what anyone would have view this situation, so that the spirit of fear would tremble. And this strange Asa also used to increase or decrease its texture and size.

Even, the place where it was kept, moved away and changed. Prophet Sueb was handed this Asa from their old legacies and instructed at the time to hand over this commodity to a high-profile prophet whenever he comes to you at the right time, it should be handed over to him.

The Valley of Tuwa

The next day, when Moses began to leave the forest with the herds of Prophet Sueb, Prophet Sueb gave some edifications.

'O, dear son! You can take these goats reeds into the forest of Madaian, whichever way you want, but in the direction of Valley of Tuwa, which is situated in the eastern, don't even wander and nobody goes there. Because that is a creepy valley and nobody used to go there. The lightning guards those creepy hills. Lightning always cracks there. So, nobody really used to go there. Besides, there are the dreaded wolves, who guard the mountain that devour those who go there, and have never returned.'

So, with these edifications, Moses left for the wilderness with the goat herd.

When Moses returned home in the evening with this clump of goats, then the Prophet Sueb's daughter welcomed Moses and old Prophet Sueb was very happy when he saw the goats being sultry.

In this way, Moses kept grazing the Prophet Sueb's goats in the forest for many years and used to feed the goats by breaking the leaves with his stick, and when the goats were grazing far and wide, he stood in a place resting on his stick. He would stand on the stick and keep eyes on the goats.

Once Moses departed on a journey to several places with goats to the forest.

On grazing the grass goat herd arrives in the distant forest, the herd of Moses' goats automatically continue to move in a particular direction.

Moses as much as possible tries to stop them, but all the goats are running away with special confinement.

If Moses stops goats from one side, goats on the other side go ahead. When Moses stops those goats, then the goats on the first side run away.

In this way, Moses is engaged in stopping every few goats, but the goat's clump was running ahead.

Finally, the goat herd reached the valley of a mountain where the ground was covered with lush green grass. When Moses inspected the surroundings, there was a great silence.

The sound of the wind blowing in this cold mountain valley came to the ears.

There was a reddish high mountain in front, but there was no one visible in this mountain valley. The sky was clear and blue. By this time, the sun was almost above the head. Somewhere in the sky, a small cloud was visible.

Everything seemed right to Moses, so Moses sat on a flat stone in the foothills.

To Moses, sitting in this little high place, the goat herd was right in front of his eyes, all the goats that had been swallowing the grass in the field, grazing the grass spread in that green grass field without any kind of hurry.

Because all the goats had come out in the long bay and this long journey had made Moses a little tired, Moses decided to rest a bit. All the goats were also visible from here.

Moses lay down keeping the stick under his head for some rest. In a short time, Moses got his eyes closed. This was a very pleasant valley. A green sabza (grass) was present all around. Herds were grazing now. Meanwhile, a large Ajdhah (Python) appeared from the red mountain in front and proceeded to swallow the goats.

It had reached to swallow the goats, then the Asa that was under Moses' head came out very precisely and turned into a big Ajdhah (Python).

His eyes were ruddy and his teeth were very big. When this celestial opened its mouth from far away, the entire area in front was filled with a balloon of fire. There was a fire on the grounds all around.

In the very next moment, this Ajdhah stood in front of that mountain Ajdhah.

Now this celestial opened his fierce mouth and breathed, then all the stones and mud started flying in the mouth of this Ajdhah.

In this way, it stood like a storm and everything lying in front of it started flying in the mouth of Ajdhah.

This Ajdhah also swallowed the mountain; Ajdhah alive. Within a short time, the entire ground was cleared, but the goats got scared after seeing this stormy scene and started running here and there.

Then that dreadful Ajdhah became the same stick again and came to Moses' bedside.

When the goats were running here and there, big wolves surrounded the herd of goats from out of the foothills of the mountain.

The goats now gathered together in one place, and in fear started shouting.

On the other hand, when it came to dusk, there was the sound of lightning on the top of that reddish mountain. At that moment, a very frightening lightning sound came into the ears of Moses, and Moses awoke from sleep.

Moses took the stick in his hand and stood up. On the top of the mysterious mountain, the lightning was howling. Moses saw the goats gathered in a frightening place.

Very dreaded wolves had surrounded the herd of goats. Now when Moses turned to the top of the mountain on standing there, he saw that electric blue circles were shining on the top of the mountain.

The sound of his crackling was causing a lot of panic. Moses kept watching this scene for a long time.

Seeing this incident, Moses considered it a privilege to leave. When Moses came toward his goats, even the fiercest wolves had escaped and disappeared into the foothills of the mountain.

Moses took his goats and ran away.

The Mount Sinai

On coming back from this dangerous journey to many places, Moses told the whole story in front of the Prophet Sueb, and then Sueb said, 'Dear Farzand! That place is Wadi-a-Tuwa and that mountain is Sinai. I have heard from my elders that there is divine manifestations sparkling there. No one has been able to bring the actual situation from there to till date and whoever went to that place, never returned. So, you too should have taken care of the edification that I had warned you about this.'

In this way, Moses completed eight years of grazing goat herds in the Prophet Sueb's favor, then Prophet Sueb had a daughter named Siphora, whose dress had opened up to Moses while bringing Moses to her home. He married her to Moses and also offered many of the goats to Moses to do it gracefully. And he said, 'O, dear Farzand! All the male goats born this year will be yours and all the female children that will be born, be mine.'

In the same way, when a year passed, then Prophet Sueb said, 'O dear Moses! This year, the number of female children of goats, those of you and all the male children, it is mine.'

Thus, Moses's goats grew to several thousand in a short period. And the tenure of the indenture became ten years instead of eight.

One day Moses, appearing in the service of Prophet Sueb, earnestly pleaded with respect, 'O respected! The feelings of love for my country draw me toward itself. If you allow me, I wish to take my wife to Egypt.'

Prophet Sueb! 'Dear Farzand! I will allow you to go to your

native country with great joy and pleasure, and I will make you move with great joy and pleasure by including a few more goats in your goat herd, along with your family.'

Including many more goats in Moses herd, willingly, his daughter Siphora and Moses, departed happily. Moses in the shadow of his God from Madaian toward a long journey to Egypt.

Moses along with thousands of goats along with his wife Sephora took the way to Egypt. On the fifth day of travel, they arrived in an unknown deep forest.

The path seemed unknown. It was getting very cold. There was a cool breeze in the evening. On the other hand, the goats used to run in a fixed direction in this cold.

Moses and Sephora would stop them at every try, but it was being dragged on an unknown path as if someone was pulling them there. Moses and his wife got tired of stopping. It was evening before they got there.

The fog had started. Sephora was shivering with cold and tightening her scarf. Now there was a mountain in front. When the cold and fog enveloped the darkness, Moses took a mountain hideout with his pregnant wife and goats. When all of them entered the mountain cave, pregnant Sephora, who had been there for all his days, had got child pain.

In this situation, Moses gave his wife a soft cloth and got up his courage, and started to make a fire by rubbing stone so that his wife could get some relief from the cold.

In this attempt, Moses hit the stone with stone to make some arrangements for the fire. But where was the fire!

In this row, he came out of the cave to have the fire, what did he see on the top of the mountain on his right side, a fire illuminated with a great swing.

Moses comes inside the cave and says to his wife – 'You

stay, I have seen the fire. Maybe I should bring some news from there or bring fire for you so that you may warm up.'

Moses took his stick in his hand and started the difficult and ugly climb of the mountain in the cold winter. The bitter cold breeze was blowing, Moses' clothes were blown off, causing more misery in this difficult path.

Holding the stones out of the mountain, Moses pressing on his stick was climbing a highly challenging height. After some time, Moses was very close to the top of the mountain. There was a deep trench below. But Moses wanted to reach this fire more quickly for his beloved wife.

Now Moses boldly reached the top of the mountain by holding pointed stones and brought his face up, only seeing the situation there, his eyes were torn.

Moses saw while hanging over the mountain that there was a fire between the shrines and bushes. When Moses came up, the hill and saw the circumstances, there was a fire between the shrines and the bushes and the twigs and shrubs of the shrine were fresh.

They were neither scorched by the fire but were refreshed and moving by the wind here and there. Moses was watching this miracle with great surprise and also a little afraid.

Moses got closer to the fire that was scattered in the twigs of the stern and when he lifted his eyes, he could see the tornado of fire was going up to the sky.

Moses saw this fire extending up to the sky, scared, he intended to move from there. At that moment, a strange voice echoed from the top of the hill and from the stern with which the fire was extracted, 'O, Moses! I am your Lord.'

Moses immediately fell on the ground in prostration. Moses sees all four directions only in prostration.

Moses mused up the courage and asked, 'Lord! Is this your voice or your prophets?'

The strange buzzing sound came –

'This is my voice, I am your Lord. So, O Moses! Remove your shoes that you are in Holy Tuwa. I have chosen you, listen to what is said.'

This voice did not coming from any particular direction, but from every convergence, Moses trembled, quickly retreated and removed his shoes, and fells back on the ground again.

Voice buzz –

'Of course, I am the God of all the universe, except me, there is no God. So, pray only for me. There is no doubt that the hour of doom is coming. I will hide it, that every person should be given his revenge and what he tries and his tries will be seen. O Moses! What is this in your right hand?'

Moses, 'This is my stick (Asa). On this, I take rest and with this, I brush leaves for my goats, and apart from this, I do many things with it.'

Divine Voice buzz, 'Put it down, O Moses!'

Moses put the stick down on the ground, and the stick moved and then turned into a big Ajdhah (Python). His eyes were shining. This Ajdhah started running with an open mouth. Moses ran back after seeing this and became frightened.

Divine Voice buzz –

'Hold it, O Moses! Do not be afraid we will return it to its first condition!'

When Moses stretched out his hand to hold on to the Ajdhah, the dreaded Ajdhah changed to his former condition as the stick and bounced back to Moses' hand.

Again Divine Voice buzz –

'Hold your right hand in your arm, O Moses! It will come

out illuminated without any defect. Again press that hand and pull it out, then it will come back to its first condition.'

When Moses held his right hand in a claw by pressing it in the arm of the left hand, it started illuminating brighter and whiter than the sunlight. When Moses again pulled it out by pressing the claw in his arm, it was in the same condition again.

Divine Voice buzz –

'Take our two signs and go to Pharaoh that he is becoming a big disobedient, talk softly, maybe he will understand and become firm.'

Moses prayed, 'My God! Open my chest, make my work easy. Open the knot of my tongue, so that they understand my point. Make one of my family members my vizier to help me, that is, my brother Aaron and to give me strength and make him a part of my work so that we can remember you a lot. There is no doubt that you see us under all circumstances.'

Divine Voice buzz –

'You are given whatever you asked for. And we have done a favor over you before that when you were on your mother's lap, we had indicated to your mother to put you in the wooden box and put it in the river then the enemy of me and you will take it out. And when your sister was saying to the people of Pharaoh, that I should show you a house that your children will be fed with milk and get well. O Moses… We brought you back to your mother to cool her eyes. Now you and your brother Aaron take the signs of our nature and go to Pharaoh and do not let our work slowdown that he has raised his head a lot. Go to him and talk to him softly, maybe, he will notice or get scared and become among the obedient.'

Moses said, 'O our God! I have murdered one of their men. I'm afraid they will kill me instead.'

Divine Voice buzz –

'O Moses! Be relaxed, we have sent you as our high and mighty prophet and strengthened you from our signs. They will not be able to control you. Go and explain to Pharaoh gently. It is not strange, he becomes among the nobles. And say that both of us have come to you, sent by your Lord, that you should not persecute Bani Israel but free them, they stay with us. Surely, I will be with you.'

Moses replied –

'O our God! When I go to my community, Bani Israel, and say that I have been sent by the God of your great grandfather, Ibrahim, Isaac, and Jacob, then if they ask me what his name then what should I tell them?'

Divine Voice buzz –

'Say this to Bani Israel: I AM WHO, I AM, the God of your father, Ibrahim, Isaac, and the Lord of Jacob, "Jehovah", He has sent me in you and behold, it will always be my name among them.'

When Moses was allowed to go from the Lord and the signs were granted, Moses returned from the top of the mountain and came back to that cave in the darkness of night where he had left his family in a delicate condition. After reaching there, he saw the cave illuminated with divine light. A lot of divine women, wearing high expensive clothes were busy looking after Siphora and a just born beautiful child was lying next to Siphora.

When he looked at the goats, big-sized wolves were protecting the goats sitting outside the cave with the most attentiveness. In this way, Moses was very delighted to see the situation in both places and because Moses was very tired now, he also rested aside in the cave there. When he woke up in the morning, told his wife –

'O Sephora! The God of Prophet Sueb has spoken to me and has appointed me as his prophet, and I have been ordered to go to Pharaoh in Egypt and speak soft things to them… Perhaps, he will give up numbness and be afraid. God has appointed my brother Aaron as my vizier in this work. So, what is your opinion about this!'

Sephora said, 'God's order is priority. So, I allow you to go to your country happily in the safety of God.'

So, both of them returned to Madaian with their goat herd. On reaching Madaian, Moses narrated all events to Prophet Sueb and asked for permission to go to Egypt alone.

Prophet Sueb replied – 'O dear Farzand! Congratulations to you, your arrival was already nominated in earlier holy books, so what orders you have given, do accordingly and those who are trapped in Bani Israel by oppressor Pharaoh, help them free and leave your family here.'

In this way, Moses departed on the road to Egypt with permission from the Prophet Sueb and Siphora with a little foodstuff for the way. Moses holding a little bit of foodstuff, carrying his stick in hand headed toward Egypt with fast steps. In this way, when Moses traveled close to Egypt while traveling on a day and night journey, the construction projects of the city of Ramesses, which were now completed, now started appearing.

The huge statue of Pyramid and Hor-e-Akhet was also visible after walking a little further.

In this way, Moses entered Egypt in the night through the huge and sky-touching statues and pillars of the city of Ramesses. Because now the beard of Moses was enlarged and it had been a long time since he had come here, there was no recognition for him in Egypt. Moses reached his mother's house in the dark of night. When Aaron, Moses' brother, had already come to know about Moses' arrival; Aaron opened the door and introduced Moses to his family.

Moses' mother, who was now old, saw Moses. There was a lot of celebration in the house.

Mother fed the two brothers. After eating the food, when all the family gathered in one place, Moses said, 'My brother Aaron! Now is not the time to sit at home. I have been granted the prophetship and have strengthened my hand by you, to send the message of the Lord to oppressor Pharaoh. It is not strange that this explanation will benefit him, and he should be among the believers and release the Bani Israel from his clutches.'

Aaron – 'O my brother Moses! Pharaoh is no longer the old Pharaoh, now he has become more bloodthirsty. Everywhere in Egypt, there is a huge scripture of Pharaoh, he forces the public to bow their head in front of them, and if they do not do so, he throws a Tauk around their neck. I am afraid that he involved us in the trial in any way.'

Moses! 'Do not be afraid, the Lord has promised me that he sees us at all times. And I have been awarded with the strong signs. They will not be able to control us. So, get up and edify people. No doubt, they accept edification, they should take the perceptibility.'

Moses at Pharaoh's Court

So, the next day Moses along with his brother Aaron reached the door of the palace of Pharaoh. So, standing in a high place, he began to edify the coming and going people!

'O, people! Jehovah has made us their prophet, so if you believe in us then there is good luck and good news for you, then pray for the one who gives livelihood to all and whatever is in between the land and the sky. The sun and the moon are following at his behest. His rule ranges from winds and seas to all land and anticipations. He laid this ground and made seven strong skies, and we all have to return to him.'

When Moses was talking about this among the people, there spread a lot of restlessness among the people gathered there. But no one dared to ask Moses anything. But a man, who was the mascot of Pharaoh's house, turned his eyes and said, 'Do you know, what place this is and what is your reason for coming here?'

Moses boldly said, 'This is the palace of Pharaoh. All of us and all humans are slaves to the master of that sky and land. Who made the day and night? And his rule is on the sea, mountains, and all the skies. The sun and the moon are roaming within a fixed radius. Day and night are put behind each other in work and each one is struggling for a time. On the day when he orders, all will be deposited in one place. Neither one clock forward nor one clock back, and that day will be ruled by him. And the person who turned his back on this edict, he became one who suffered heavy losses.'

Hearing this, he ran away inside the palace with an open mouth. Going inside the palace, that mascot of Pharaoh's house went close to Pharaoh Ramesses and said, 'Today, I have brought a piece of strange news. Dare not say!'

Pharaoh (strangely)! 'What's that?'

Mascot! 'Those two men who are sitting at the door of the palace, the lions dare due to their habitation. They say that there is another Lord except you who is the creator of land and sky. And the only order of him is to follow. He is the master of all livelihood.'

While saying this, the mascot trembled.

Pharaoh grudgingly ordered Haman to spot both of them in the court.

When a grand door of the palace opened, the vizier of the palace told Moses and Aaron the royal decree – 'You have the royal command to hold you in the royal court!'

So, they took Moses and Aaron in the circle and walked toward the court of Pharaoh.

That huge door of the palace automatically closed as soon as they entered the door.

There were large statues on both sides of the road that were shining in golden color. Behind the idols were very high statues with many pictures inscribed in the hieroglyphs.

Moving on, a wall appeared on which the hieroglyphs were painted showing the court of Pharaoh, and Pharaoh and his queen were shown sitting on a high throne.

Both Moses and Aaron, who were walking close to each other, when approaching the wall, saw the wall become two parts to the left and right. In front, there was the bird's eye court of Pharaoh. Pillars of light touching the sky. Amongst the larger scriptures of preceding Pharaoh, there was a throne of Pharaoh at a high place in front.

Pharaoh was wearing Nemes, a large square woolen cloth folded diagonally worn across the forehead, and wearing a crown of Upper and Lower Egypt, double crown the Pschent in great glory. He was also wearing a plunging necklace of gold blue and black beetles around the neck and an amulet, believed to protect and give the strength carrying Hekha-Nekhakha in his hands.

Near the throne, Queen Isetnofret was sitting most proudly, wearing a golden straight dress with two shoulder straps held by two golden strips and worn down to the ankle with a neck collar with bright color beads and a cobra crown on the head.

On one side of the throne, there were huge gold statues of Gods Ra and Hathor, on the other side golden idols of Osiris, Isis, and Horus were shining.

When both of them came forward in the court, Pharaoh and Queen Isetnofret saw two men wearing thicker and longer fabric and standing awake and scared next to each other. There were shoes on their feet. Everyone was watching them both. Nobody dared to speak.

Vizier Haman (sobbing)! 'You are in the court of Pharaoh, the great and do not bow down.'

Moses! 'We bow only before the master of the land and the sky. No longer ahead of slaves.'

All courtiers became a restless marvel.

Now the Pharaoh recognized the voice and the Queen Isetnofret also recognized it, so the trouble arose, but she was forced in front of Pharaoh.

Pharaoh said, 'What is your name?'

Moses, 'Moses bin Amran.'

All courtiers, Haman, Amun, everyone was shocked. Pharaoh said, 'I do not ask this.'

Moses said, 'I am one of the captives of God.'

Pharaoh said, 'I don't even ask this.'

Moses! 'We have been given a message for you, that you should accept the master of the land and the sky as your God and do not turn your face and be in the firm.'

Pharaoh said, 'You must say that I am one of the slaves of Pharaoh. I am raised by him. He has much favor over me. He owes me a lot. O Moses! Are you not the one to whom I have given shelter? But you have perished. And apart from this, you did a job that you know very well. Now from where did you get this high status that you come here to advise me?'

Moses said, 'I had raised my hand to end the quarrel. How did I know that he would die? And killing like this, the fine does not apply. And you intended that, due to enmity, I was intent to kill. So, I could not compete with you and for fear of your oppression, I got down from here and took the path of the deep forest. The God of all has done me a great favor to give me a place to stay in Madaian. He called me on Mount Sinai, and has given me strong signs and granted me the prophetship and strengthened my arm with this my brother and made him my vizier. We have a message for you; you have spread the very open violence in the ground, and you are getting very undutiful. It is an offer for you to give up your insistence and release Bani Israel from your oppression and accept the owner of the land and sky as your God and not turn your face.'

Hearing this, the senses of all the courtiers kept going but the Queen Isetnofret was very happy.

Aaron! 'O Pharaoh! Strangely, you criticize for the killing of a man, while for the last seventy years, countless sons of Bani Israel have been murdered and brutally oppressed by you. Their old and pregnant have been deployed to wipe stones from mines, kept hungry, and done the hardest work, and weakened Bani Israel so much that they cannot even raise their heads. You don't see these conditions. Now it is appropriate for you to accept one God and release Bani Israel from your oppression.'

Pharaoh said, (Awesomely) 'If both of you have laid down to someone other than me, then I imprison you both now and punish you to death right now.'

Moses said, (In anger) 'I see that you are impotent in an open guise, you cannot do anything to us, because the Lord has sent us with strong signs.'

Pharaoh said, ' If you are truthful then show your sign.'

Moses then put his stick (Asa) on the ground. It was immediately transformed into a ferocious Ajdhah (Python). The dreaded Ajdhah gradually grew. Now this disaster raised its mouth, and the watchers became conscious. Ajdhah was still becoming increasingly large.

Now his hiss was also starting to be heard. Lightning began to crack through his eyes. People started running away and the courtiers sought refuge. A heavy storm was wrecked in the court of Pharaoh.

When this dreaded Ajdhah opened its mouth, many huge statues standing there caught fire. The luxurious palace of Pharaoh started burning in fire.

There was a stampede in the court. Haman and Amun backed away in fear, that the dreadful Ajdhah had started destroying the palace. An earthquake had occurred in the court of Pharaoh.

Now the dreaded Ajdhah turned toward Pharaoh and opened his mouth, it had seemed that it would swallow this entire palace.

Now Pharaoh panicked and shouted! 'Moses; Stop this disaster.'

Moses extended his right hand toward Ajdhah, and then the

dreaded Ajdhah, whose head was going to the top of the palace, fell into the hand of Moses and became the same stick.

The fire in the palace was still on. When the chaos slowly subsided, the rest of the courtiers came forward in fear, all covered with dust.

Pharaoh and Queen Isetnofret were sitting on their throne frightened.

Pharaoh was terrified.

Moses came ahead and asked Pharaoh 'I keep one more symbol of my prophetship.'

Pharaoh (afraid) said, 'What is that?'

Moses took his right hand in the armpit and then pulled it out, it started shining like sunlight. Such a light was bursting from this that the eyes could not see this.

The whole palace of Pharaoh shone with that light. The people wanted refuge again. So, Moses pressed his hand in the side and pulled it out, then it was the same.

Moses turned to both of them and asked, 'Now what is your intention!'

Pharaoh said, 'O Moses, what will I get in return if I agree with you and bring trust in your God?'

Moses said, 'O Pharaoh! If you have been lobbying me and accept faith, then you have the good news of four things.

'One – for you is everlasting youth, you will never grow old.

'Two – that you get such sovereignty that no one else can take away.

'Three – that you should always be healthy and you never get sick.

'Four – that Heaven always comes in your part.'

Hearing this, he said, 'Moses! Today, you both go, I will look into your offer, and I will talk to my sensible people and then shall answer.'

So, first, he went to the palace and took advice from his Queen Isetnofret.

Queen Isetnofret said, 'O Pharaoh! no intelligent person will let such values go with his hands. So, do not delay and immediately obey Moses.'

Then he went aside and advises with Vizier Haman.

Haman (making a bad mouth) said, 'It is very strange that till now you are sitting on a throne and all worship you and now you will adopt someone else's lobbying. Did you not see that Moses had been missing from here for so many days and came to learn a heavy spell and wanted, with the power of his magic, to take this country from you and expel you from your country.'

Pharaoh's mind turned to reverse.

Pharaoh said, 'O Haman! the greed of everlasting youth and everlasting sovereignty made me crazy. So, O Haman! What is your opinion on this matter?'

Haman! 'At this moment, keep the case of Moses and his brother delayed and leave messengers in the country. Moses is a magician. So, call the great magicians of the country. They will confront Moses and defeat Moses with their heavy magic.'

Pharaoh liked this advice. He ordered! 'Immediately send messengers to a deaf country to call famous magicians to appear in the palace of Pharaoh and show their amazing feats and defeat Moses in magic, then enter the courts (honors) in the court of the Pharaoh.'

One day, Moses and Aaron appeared at the Pharaoh's court in the presence of Vizier Haman, Amun, and other courtiers and pleaded.

Moses, 'O Pharaoh! what is the delay in this, that you can defend me and be in the believers?'

Haman! 'O Moses! You are not that who was nothing. Who found a place in the house of great Pharaoh, well, brought up, even reached youth, then one day ran away after doing a misfortune that was not appropriate to you. You remain missing from here for so many days and have come by learning a heavy spell. Now with the help of its magic, you want to snatch Pharaoh's country and dishonor him out of his country.'

Pharaoh was in pleasure to listen to these clever pleas of Haman and sat on his throne in swag.

Moses and Aaron got very angry after hearing these words of Haman.

Pharaoh assented and challenged Moses to a kind of duel set for a day of the festival.

'O Moses! So why not put a challenge of magic and what is proved, that should be implemented. And on the day of the festival, everyone should gather in the field and see who remains the winner.'

Moses and the Challenge of the Magicians

Courtiers were sent to spot the brightest magician to reach Pharaoh's court on the day of the festival from all of Egypt. These courtiers, covering thousands of expert sorcerers and their magic items, reached a colony where two real brothers lived who had a big name in magic.

So, the courtiers wanted to take both of them together. They reached the colony of both expert magicians.

Then the two brothers were told about Moses and Aaron and their strange and powerful Asa (stick) situation in front of them.

'O our masterful Egyptian wizards! Two men have come to the court of our and your Lord great Pharaoh, who, with the help of their magic, want to expel our God-Pharaoh from his country. Although both of them are completely empty handed, they have a stick (Asa) which is very strange and distinguished. When they put it on the ground, it becomes a very terrible and ferocious Ajdhah, and after that whatever is in front of him, he swallows it all in a moment. Nothing can stand in front of him. Because there is no other couple in Egypt than you in an exceptional job, you have to come to us; beat them both in magic and gain a place of glory in the court of the God-Pharaoh.'

Hearing the circumstances of Moses and that dreaded Ajdhah, they both said, 'We are not ready for the contest right now... You just wait.'

Leaving the group of the courtiers and all the other magicians there, they both left and entered a hut. There they told the whole story to his old mother.

So, the old mother opened a strange box in one corner of the hut and took out something wrapped in red cloth, and came out of the settlement with both her sons.

After going to an old tomb there and opening a red cloth, there were some plates on which something was written in Hieroglyphs.

This tomb belonged to the father of these two boys, who had been dead a long time, and the old mother opened the tablets and read some magic words. Then a blue shadow emerged on that grave and a boy gave a voice.

'O our father! Today, we have stuck into a problem; the king of Egypt has summoned us to his palace where there are two people who have neither any goods nor any equipment... just a stick, and when they put it on the ground, it becomes a furious Ajdhah and all that it has in front, becomes its morsel.

'The motto of Pharaoh is to challenge that radical thing with expert wizards and beat that disaster with the help of magic.'

On hearing this incident from the child, there was silence for a while. Then, from the blue shadow that dominated over the tomb, a loud voice came – 'My children! You must go there and, surely, go there and intelligently verify that when the owner of that stick (Asa) falls asleep, does it still become an Ajdhah. If you get the news that it becomes Ajdhah even after, they are asleep, then be assured that it is not such a magical thing, then it is a Gabi Asrar and that has no match. And then incline toward the owner of the Asa, notice that he praises himself and talks proudly with rotating eyes, then there is no harm to confront him. You will overcome it. If he speaks softly and directly, talks about goodness, then remember that it is compulsory for you to follow him and that even the most amazing magicians of the world cannot overcome him.'

The loud voice became silent.

The old mother along with her children withdrew from there and came home and gathered seventy-two disciples, who were their companions in the magic. And with all of them, they left for Egypt with their distinguished pieces of equipment of magic.

When the day of the competition came, its fame was far and wide. Millions of people began to gather to see this strange spectacle. At the bottom of the palaces of Pharaoh was a large ground that was chosen for this contest.

From one side, the great pyramid of Egypt and the huge statue of Hor-e-Akhet were visible, on the other side, the new city of Ramesses was looking very miraculous in golden shadow.

On the western side of the ground, was the huge golden throne for seating of Pharaoh and Queen Isetnofret, behind which and on both sides, sculptures of earlier Pharaohs, with deities and divine powers, were installed.

On the backside, there were large sets of sculptures with Gods and celestial powers also shown. In front of all this, there was an open field where the competition was to be held.

On three sides of this ground, there were the sitting types of stairs to sit on for the Egyptian crowd.

Thus, there was a crowd that gathered and the field was filled with people. Then thousands of magicians with their furnishings in that ground descended.

A corps of magicians descends there, holding ropes and bamboos in the hands of the master magicians, and some holding tree branches in the hands.

There were some magicians there, among them, few were only keeping an eye on the sky. There was no looking here or there. Some people do not lift their eyes above the ground, then some people come to make a strange appearance with closed eyes.

In this way, the large groups of magicians made the field full of ropes, wood, and other accessories.

When the big moment arrived, Pharaoh, Queen Isetnofret, Vizier Haman, Amun, and the higher-ranked wizards of the royal court, entered the premises and were seated on their throne. The ground was surrounded by stepped seating stalls on three sides up to as far as the eye see. The field was filled with people.

Now they were waiting for Moses to come. After some time Moses appeared, wearing thick woolen clothes, shoes on feet, and his stick in hand with his brother Aaron approaching in the field. They entered the ground with lowered eyes. Moses and Aaron entered the field with intermittent steps and stood on one side.

Millions of spectators were consulting amongst themselves.

Well, these two empty-handed men, dressed in thick clothes, will they be able to combat the magicians? Those who have come with the accessories of heavy magic.

Thousands of magicians gathered there and turned their eyes on Moses and Aaron, and they were not surprised to see Moses and Aaron. They were looking at Moses with crooked hair on their mouths and an illusion of not seeing him. So, a small group came forward in the midst of magicians and bowed down to the throne.

Again among the magicians, another group came forward and bowed down to the throne. Then that experienced team raised their hands toward Pharaoh and prayed.

'O our God-Pharaoh! What would your boon be if we prevail over Moses? And we hope that we will be able to stand by the glory of great Pharaoh.'

Haman (in a raised voice)! 'Pharaoh guarantees that your

place is secure with him, a proximity that comes with inducements and untold perks for you all.'

Magicians fell to the ground, bowing their heads in front of Pharaoh. And getting up, came forward with great strut and badness toward the place where Moses and Aaron were standing silently and walked ahead.

While facing Moses – 'O Moses! If you win today, we will defend you, but we hope that we will be able to succeed by the might of Pharaoh.'

Moses on referring to magicians! 'O, dear brothers! We have neither come to you with any magic nor have we come here of our own free will. The creator of this land and sky has sent us toward you; by making us his prophet by giving us the strong sign to proclaim the good news and fear, and has given a strong message for those who wanted to walk on the right path, and the one who turned his face, became a loser. So, the prayer belongs to the one who owns the land, sky, night and day, mountains and sea.

'He is the one who made the ground plain for you people and released the paths in it and made the sky stand up with no pillars and made it rain and created various things in it so that you can take advantage of them. Death is confirmed. Ultimately, everyone will return to God. So, whoever has to think, think what he has done for the afterlife.'

The group of magicians were surprised to hear these simple and flat things from Moses.

He did not talk about his greatness nor did he talk roundly. Both the sorcerers (magician brothers) remembered the advice of their father Marhoom. Those masterful sorcerers came in sweat and kept looking at Moses with their mouths open. Hearing these edifications from Moses, there were other magicians who had still not even opened their eyes, who now opened them, and looked at Moses with astonishment and began to quarrel among themselves.

Then one of them said, 'These two are magicians. They want to expel you from your country on the basis of their magic. So, the one who will be successful today is succeeded.'

Then a group of magicians came forward and said to Moses, 'O Moses! This is the reason for us and you to gather in this place today, so why don't you cast your spell. If you win, we promise that we will all defend you. So, Moses put yours first or we'll put something in the field.'

Moses said, 'You cast first.'

So, this group of magicians put round rings in the field and made some gestures to those rings, then these rings started rotating in the field.

The ground was filled with these rings by moving around. Now these rings started moving up and moving fast.

The rings got up in the sky on that ground and then made a cyclone like that. This cyclone took up all the sand in the field. Now the magicians created a huge storm of sand there. In this storm, the sound of lightning started coming. Now a storm of dust moved ahead to take the spectators in the cyclone.

Dust was blowing everywhere. Nothing was visible. Just the terrible sound of this storm and the sound of thunderous thunder in it was shaking all the spectators present there with fear. What was the magic there? A quandary was created.

At one time, it seemed that this sand storm would take all the ground to the sky; Pharaoh and Haman also saw that the storm's edge had reached the clouds above the sky.

Now the observers felt that this cyclone would pick them up from this place and take them to the sky, then there was a big noise among the spectators.

Seeing this, a chief magician of the staff who had raised both his hands shook them down, and then the whole balloon of sand came onto the ground and disappeared completely. The spectators who were sitting with their hands on their heads hidden till now started to look around with surprise.

There was no sign of dust and soil.

Seeing the feats of the magicians, Pharaoh, Haman, and Amun grew up and looked at Moses with grief.

Then another group of magicians came forward, put a pot of water in the ground, and made a gesture to it with hands and eyelids, and some fumes came out of that pot and went into the sky and started moving in the sky.

Now this fume enveloped the sky so much that the whole sky was filled with clouds, lightning started flashing intermittently.

And the wind started blowing on that ground. Then the wind slowly took the form of a storm. Then it started raining heavily with strong lightning.

People ran toward the shadows to avoid this rain. People's hearts were being shaken by lightning. They clamped their ears with their hands.

Some covered their heads in their hands to avoid the rain but what? It was raining heavily on their heads but not a single drop was falling on the ground. Everything was dry on the ground!

So, the magicians surprised the people by showing huge magic. After this, another group of magicians came out of their line, and they put large cords and sticks in the ground, then made the gestures with the fingers and eyelids in such a way that the cords and sticks started elongating and rising.

Right in front of their eyes, the whole field was filled with big man-headed large scorpions and terrible Ajdhah.

Now these terrible scorpions and Ajdhahs started moving here and there in the field and a lot of heavy fighting started between them.

A fierce battle ensued between terrible scorpions and Ajdhahs. From these scorpions and Ajdhahs limbs began to fall between the spectators. Now the Army of these man-faced scorpions that were fighting in the field turned toward the spectators sitting, they shouted in astonishment, they were shocked. There was a huge noise among the spectators. Spectators started shouting.

The magicians brought amazing magic and their magic worked on the hearts of people. These big scorpions even frightened Moses and Aaron who felt that now these big scorpions and Ajdhah were about to attack them. Moses' brother Aaron was so scared that he grabbed the shoulder of Moses and realized the fear. Now the Pharaoh and Haman were very happy to see this witchcraft.

The Queen Isetnofret, who was sitting in a little distance of Pharaoh, seemed a bit restless looking at this machination of magicians. Moses placed the palm of his hand on Aaron's palm which was on the shoulder of Moses and gave courage to Aaron.

In a state of great anger, this time Moses threw away his Asa (stick) over to the ground.

The ground started shaking as soon as it touched the ground. Asa started to raise and changed into a dreaded Ajdhah and started to rise, with lightning eyes, the hearts of spectators were being stopped by the breath of this Ajdhah.

The Ajdhah moved a little forward and rose. As soon as it opened its mouth, the ground started shaking, there was burning all around the field.

The dreaded storm started moving. Fire raining from its mouth started. A fire broke out in sculptures and big idols of Pharaoh and other Gods above the ground and started burning with huge smoke all around.

Seeing this view, the spectators' senses flew away. Now this celestial breathed inside, so many of the celestial and human-faced scorpions in the field started flying into the mouth of this celestial one.

Due to the breathing of this Ajdhah, there was a storm in the ground. Wherever Ajdhah opens his mouth, everything would fly to his mouth, and there was a huge stampede in the field. Spectators felt that now they are going to become a meal of this disaster, then there was chaos there. People started running from their places with their feet over each other. There was a scream among them. The Ajdhah still stood in the field with an open mouth.

When all the wizards of the magicians and all the scorpions and all their belongings went to the mouth of this disaster, then it turned to the other side of the field, so there the stones, statues, and buildings of the temple flew into the mouth of that dreaded Ajdhah.

When the ground was cleared of everything, Ajdhah turned to the Pharaoh and Queen Isetnofret. Where the dreadful bearers on both sides of Pharaoh's throne were tied in the chain of iron, the chains broke down, becoming the morsel of that Ajdhah.

The big sculptures that were installed on both sides of the throne also broke down and fell in the mouth of the Ajdhah. Now this disaster opened the mouth to swallow Pharaoh and Queen Isetnofret, with its hands' long teeth.

It was near to swallowing all of them when Haman shouted, 'O great Pharaoh! Save us from this disaster.' Haman clung to the feet of the Pharaoh.

When the Pharaoh saw this terrible wrecking close to him, immediately with anger, he took out his celestial weapon the golden spear of Osiris, and quickly opened it and aimed it toward the Ajdhah.

Immediately getting up from the throne, Queen Isetnofret came in the middle of that Pharaoh and terrible Ajdhah.

Queen Isetnofret ordered Moses, 'Moses! I order you to stop this wrecking!'

At this voice, Moses opened his hand toward the scary Ajdhah, it immediately collapsed into the same stick and bounced off in the hand of Moses.

And the ground was absolutely clean from the machination of magicians. At the same time, in one corner, there was panic and magicians stood with each other, tongued and frightened. The magicians understood that Moses was not a magician.

Magicians fell to their faces in prostration and declared their belief in the unseen Lord of the worlds, the Lord of Moses and Aaron

So, they replied to Moses – 'We bring belief to the Lord of Moses and Aaron and are among the believers.'

When Pharaoh saw that all the magicians had brought their belief to the Lord of Moses, he became very furious in the presence of his all courtiers.

Pharaoh said with great anger, 'Before I allow you, you all bring your belief to the God of Moses. Of course, he is the elder of all of you and it is all your collusion. If you all don't leave your belief from Moses, remember that I will cut off several limbs on opposite sides, and crucify all of you on the palm trees.'

The magicians replied, 'O Pharaoh! Now we have nothing to do with your presence and your outbreaks. Ultimately, one day we will return to God, should we go back on the righteous thing when it has come to us.'

Haman (bitterly)! 'Of course, Moses is the master of all of you. This all is your collusion, and you all have learned this intelligence from him.'

The magicians restated their resolve and affirmed it regardless of what they were forced to endure.

Then Moses said to the scared group, 'You all trust in faith and be a stepping stone and trust your God, there will be no difficulty left, and you will be counted among the most successful and obedient and this is the open success forever.'

Then Pharaoh proudly addressed his courtiers! 'O my courtiers! I do not see any other God except me, and Moses gives the mark of an unseen sky God, then, O Haman! fire the mud and build a high building so that I can climb on it and reach the God of Moses. Let it be decided between me and him.'

Thus, millions of slaves were put into a project, and the construction of a very big luxurious building was started. It was a skyscraper whose height was so high that the uppermost urn was beyond the clouds.

When this magnificent lime building was ready, Pharaoh went to see this building with the fearful Haman, and after seeing that building, Pharaoh thought that when he reached its height, I would surely reach the sky.

Pharaoh arrived at that dizzying building with Haman. There, he entered an octagonal geometric structure inside the building to go up. Near the building some skilled personnel connected to some construction projects were operating some crucial operations at the bottom floor, the hexagonal structure started to rise rapidly from the pressure of water. Under that geometric structure, the water starts filling up very fast, similarly, the hexagonal structure was rising up inside that building as fast.

Like this, the door opens up on both sides of the geometric structure quickly after going to the maximum top.

Both Pharaoh and Haman when walking out, found themselves in the clouds. When they looked down, the great River Nile was looking just like a blue thin stripe. The building was so high that the huge and great palace of Pharaoh looked very tiny from there. The sculptures of the Pharaoh's palace were hardly visible, the pyramids and Hor-e-Akhet, were visible only when focusing on them and looked very small in size. The view of the populated city of Ramesses was reflecting a very panoramic view from this clouds-touching erection. The green agricultural fields and date gardens on both sides of the blue River Nile were scattering a very pleasant view.

As Pharaoh turned his eyes toward the sky. So, the sky was equally distant as it was visible from the ground.

Pharaoh looked at Haman, Haman turned his eyes down. He did not have answers to these questions.

Then Pharaoh in anger took out that divine spear of Osiris and opened its arms in full, he threw it up in the sky. When that divine trident started rising up in the sky, it caught fire in a few moments.

As this weapon rose high in the sky, it became hot and turned red. The red hot spear was still rising, suddenly, it was struck by lightning from the sky, and the weapon shattered into pieces with a blast. Then the same lightning came forward and struck on that towering erection where the Pharaoh and Haman stood above and watching. With a blast, the bastions of the erection bounced off in the air.

Meanwhile, Haman pulled the Pharaoh into the geometric structure that brought them up.

The door closed automatically as Haman and Pharaoh fell inside the geometric structure. The hexagonal structure started falling down rapidly. The construction experts had realized the situation above. Instant bumps of water were opened together, through which water was coming out at a very large volume.

The faster the water was coming out, the faster the geometric structure was coming down. And the whole building was also rapidly falling apart from the top. The geometric structure fell rapidly and fell into a large chamber of water and that grand erection broke down and scattered in pieces.

There was just a big dust cloud there all around. In a little while, when this balloon of dust disappeared, then that hexagonal geometric structure was seen floating over the water.

Seeing all these extraordinary eventualities, Ankhenamesh, who was the chief architect of huge temples, power columns, and other extraordinary construction projects of Egypt, became more convinced with Moses that there is definitely an external force that is helping Moses all the time. Which has enough power that this great erection got turned into dust in a moment. Definitely, this is possible to a great divine power only.

Then one day, Ankhenamesh collected his community and told them – 'O my community! You are among a very foolish and hard-hearted people on this earth. You saw so many of Moses spectacles and miracles and kept turning your face and hardening your heart from his side and did not obey Moses, your persecution of the people of Bani Israel is increasing, so why don't you understand?'

Hearing this from Ankhenamesh, the man of his community ran to the court of Pharaoh.

The man from Ankhenamesh community! 'O great Pharaoh! Ankhenamesh has shown his belief in the God of Moses. He refuses to consider you as the greatest God of us, and he is provoking your community against you.

'He says that I will consider whom as my God who enters day into the night and night into the day and life and death are in his hand.'

Ankhenamesh was called upon in the full court of the great Pharaoh.

Haman (along with cleverly)! 'O our dear brother Ankhenamesh! Have you come to the fabricated trap of Moses? This man of your community says that you refuse to accept the great Pharaoh as your God.'

Ankhenamesh! 'O Haman! Don't you see with your own eyes that the radical erections made by you, which we took a long time to build, using millions of skilled workmen, symmetrical form, the rhythm of design, took off in the air in an instant? So, this work can be easy only for exceptional power. And you also saw that the great Pharaoh was unable to stop that big destruction in front of their eyes.'

Haman! 'That is you refusing to accept the great Pharaoh as your God.'

Ankhenamesh (looking toward the great Pharaoh)! 'I shall consider whom, as my God, who kills and resurrects, who has the monitoring of death and life in his hands.'

Haman (with bitter mouth)! 'All these works adorn to the great Pharaoh, and you have committed the disgrace of the great Pharaoh in his court, and you will see that its punishment is death.'

Haman pointed to the soldiers, to capture Ankhenamesh.

Ankhenamesh (strictly to Vizier Haman)! 'O Haman! Haven't you heard what I said? Life and death are not in the hands of you, Amun and Pharaoh.'

In that moment, Ankhenamesh carried an octagonal device in his hand and some of the petals opened out of it from which dark blue and ruddy lights were scattering out.

Now Ankhenamesh put that device down there on the colorful flower on the floor. As soon as the device was placed on a flower made of stone, both device and flower started rotating on their axis, then the flower incorporated that device in a very strange way. Both the device and the flower together formed a unique flower shape. The whole court was looking at this manifestation of Ankhenamesh.

Pharaoh, Queen Isetnofret, Vizier Haman, Amun, and all the courtiers in court were observing the wonder with great surprise. Ankhenamesh took two steps ahead and stood on that flower. Then the flower had some mechanical actions and started rotating their petals in opposite directions to each other and opened strangely and started taking Ankhenamesh into itself.

Ankhenamesh started going vertically into the flower.

In a moment, Ankhenamesh completely disappeared into the flower on the floor, then the flower turned around fantastically and became the flower of its original shape.

When the soldiers of the palace threw their hands on that flower, nothing happened and that flower was only a flower on the floor.

Pharaoh, Queen Isetnofret, Vizier Haman, Amun, and all the courtiers in court became very frightened to see the circumstances.

Haman (becoming angry over soldiers)! 'Ankhenamesh's mind is unmatched in mechanics, so you go and capture him alive and present him in the court of Pharaoh soon.'

Haman then turns toward the Pharaoh and says, 'O Pharaoh! Will you leave Moses open in your country just to spoil your religion and trick people like this, and create a mess in your fantastic religion?'

Amun – 'O our God-Pharaoh! Now the water is above the head. Now you should sacrifice Moses and all his community so that there should be no scope of it that someone will spoil this great religion of yours.'

After listening to all, the arguments among the courtiers Pharaoh ordered (in great anger and frustration)! 'This is the order of Pharaoh, the palace is to light a big heavy fire and heat the oil in big pots, and those who refused to inscribe the great Pharaoh as their greatest God, should be poured into the boiling oil.'

Queen Isetnofret (standing together angrily)! 'O Pharaoh! Why do you fall into the misery and misguidedness of your courtiers, and take the path of misleading? Moses is the prophet of God. You cannot spoil him because he has been sent with a great charter. Do you not understand?'

Then the Pharaoh said to Queen Isetnofret – 'O Isetnofret! Have you also brought your belief in Moses? If this is the fact, then return from the religion of Moses… otherwise, I will first make you involved in very tough astonishment. If you remain away from the religion of Moses, then I will build palaces of gold and silver for you, and you will be happy. If you refuse me, I will pull your skin and make you die in huge trouble.'

Queen Isetnofret! 'O Pharaoh! These gold and silver jewels are just for this world only, and we all have to return to the same God who owns this world and the next world. O Pharaoh! I have nothing to do with you any more. From today onwards, I take a separate route from your beauty, and my and your ways are different now.'

Hearing this reply of Queen Isetnofret, Pharaoh was very

worried and apprehensively ordered! 'Queen Isetnofret should be taken into custody so that she might think, it is not surprising that she will turn from its insistence and obey me.'

When Queen Isetnofret did not listen to Pharaoh, then he increased the oppression against Queen Isetnofret.

Even after many persecutions like this, when Queen Isetnofret did not move from the belief of Moses, one day those bloodthirsty ordered Queen Isetnofret to lie down in the wooden trunk, put iron nails in her hands and made her stand in front of the Egyptian people. Queen Isetnofret's blood was falling from her hands and feet on the ground, she was a weak hearted woman, facing a tough test.

Pharaoh once again came forward and asked the queen, 'Isetnofret, I still have ease for you, if you still come back from the unseen God of Moses and Aaron you can get rid of this stiff pain and be released from my tough grip.'

Queen Isetnofret! 'Why should I fear this torture and sufferings? While my venerable God has prepared for me forever green gardens and cold canals near him, which never go away. So, you turn away from me.'

Hearing this, Pharaoh became more alarmed and said, 'A heavy stone should be placed on the chest of this undutiful so that its work can be done all away.'

Queen Isetnofret, raising her eyes toward the sky! 'O my venerable! build a house for me in paradise, I am a woman, I cannot tolerate much stiff suffering. Give me relief from the torture of oppressor Pharaoh.'

At the same time, Queen Isetnofret had been shown her heavenly castle and fortalice from her eyes and saw the very pleasant breeze and the glowing illumination coming from there, on her. When Queen Isetnofret had seen the raining of all those blessings, she forgot all sorrows and troubles and smiled. And then the spirit of Queen Isetnofret departed from her body toward paradise instantly.

The conditions of the scenario when seen by the people of Egypt who were present there, made the hearts of many of them bow down to the faith of Queen Isetnofret, and their hearts became very sorrowful.

One of them started saying, 'It is something that the Queen Isetnofret did not fall from her faith even after bearing such a tough torture from Pharaoh.'

So, they also removed the fear of Pharaoh from their heart and returned to strengthen his hearts.

Then they went to Moses and recited the whole story of Queen Isetnofret by weeping tearfully. On hearing, Moses' heart was filled with sorrow. Moses began to think, 'The mother who raised me lovingly from my childhood to my youth, gave me a place in her lap, raised me, supported me in every trouble, and now she got so much pain from the bloodthirsty.'

Moses filled with rage and anger and stretched out his hand toward the sky with Asa in one hand.

I Curse – Locusts. Then in the far sky, deep and dense darkness throughout the land was seen coming toward Egypt. At that time, the Egyptians were busy taking care of their orchards and broad crops on the banks of the Nile. It was a pleasant sunny day, Incense was blooming, and date trees were full of dates. Then there was dense darkness throughout the land of Egypt. People were standing there watching this eventuation, feeling some frightening sounds, that together the swarms of locusts broke on those crops and over them.

Suddenly, when the Egyptians fled they, saw the disaster on their heads, and that terrible tornado of locusts covered everyone there.

The locusts came up over the whole land of Egypt and settled down over all its territory. Never before had there been such a fierce swarm of locusts, nor will there ever be again. They covered the surface of the whole land so that it became black. They ate up all the vegetation in the land and all the fruit of the trees the hail had spared. Nothing green was left on any tree or the plants in the fields throughout the land of Egypt. In a few moments, this disaster from the sky began to rip all the agricultural land of Egypt as well as the wooden furnishings inside the houses and palaces. Locusts ripped up the skin of the people working in their fields.

The palace of Pharaoh himself was also under arrest in this sky swarms of locusts. They ate up the remnant saved in the houses, as well as all the trees that were growing in the fields.

But every house and man of Bani Israel was safe from this sky swarms of locusts.

After seeing this situation for three days, Egyptians, with blood flowing from the bodies that were consumed by the swarms of locusts, came to Moses crying and began to complain —

'O Moses! We have sinned against the Lord, your God, and you. But now, forgive our sin only once, and pray to your God to take this death from us. You see our fields and gardens are all ruined. And we and our children are stunned in stiff trouble. If you relieve us from this disaster, then we promise that we will leave Pharaoh and believe in the God of Moses and Aaron.'

Hearing these statements of the Egyptians, Moses went with them to the wilderness where the whole area was completely covered by the swarms of locusts.

Egyptians also reached there fearfully behind Moses. After

reaching there, Moses saw the scene there and raised his Asa toward those clusters of locusts, that huge cluster of locusts got divided into two parts simultaneously.

One part flew into the sky in one Simtha (direction), the other part to the second Simtha. The swarm of these locusts blew from there, the dark shadow in the sky slowly began to be trimmed and brightened. The wind hurled all those clusters of locusts into the Red Sea.

Now they looked at the orchard and farming there, that the clusters of locusts not only littered the farming and produce but also the meat from all the stables and the humans present there.

Then soon the sun started to appear. Moses now turned to Egyptians with them and asked, 'What do you feel about your promise?'

They replied, 'Moses! We have seen such magic before also. Now your ways and ours are separated.' And they all turned away.

Like that, when that curse of the locusts from Egypt went away from them and the people turned away from believing in the God of Moses and Aaron,

II Curse – Lice. Then a month later, Moses and Aaron went to Pharaoh and asked him, 'O Pharaoh! Let my people go to serve their Lord. If you refuse to let them go, then God will send a curse of lice over all your territory. God will send swarms of flies and lice upon you and your servants and your people and your houses.

Pharaoh, however, hardened his heart and would not listen to them and ordered them to leave the palace.

Then in anger, Moses and Aaron left Pharaoh's palace and reached in the plan, stretched out his hand with his Asa, and struck the dust of the earth, in an instant lice came upon human beings and beast alike. All the dust of the earth turned into gnats and lice throughout the land of Egypt. The lice were on human beings and beast alike, and the magicians said to Pharaoh, 'This is the finger of God.' The houses of the Egyptians and the very ground on which they stood filled with swarms of gnats and lice. But on that day, an exception was on the land of Goshen, where the people of Bani Israel were, no swarms of lice were there, it rained like a machete and shattered the Egyptian heads and mouths.

With this wonder, Egyptians shouted and then went to Pharaoh and pleaded to weep.

A weak man came forward and urged Pharaoh – 'O Pharaoh! We have got trapped in stiff trouble, Moses and Aaron have ruined our lives and our beasts alike with their great magic. Why do you not rid of us of this hail? Thick swarms of lice entered in the houses of your people throughout the land of Egypt, the land is devastated on account of lice.'

Then Pharaoh summoned Moses and Aaron and said, 'O Moses! Go sacrifice to your God within the land. I will let you go to sacrifice to your God, in the wilderness, provided that you do not go too far away. Pray for us.'

Moses answered, 'As soon as I leave you I will pray to the God that the swarms of lice may depart tomorrow from Pharaoh, his servants, and his people.' When Moses left Pharaoh, he prayed to God and asked, removing the swarms of lice from Pharaoh, his servants, and his people.

When the Egyptians saw Moses raise his hand and made him move his wonders, not one louse remained. The Egyptians were very happy. One of them started saying, 'Now we are convinced that there is no other person than Moses who specializes in the magic on this land, through which he is hurting us in various ways.' And all the Egyptians returned from there to make a bitter face. And once more Pharaoh became obstinate and would not let the people of Bani Israel go.

III Curse – The Frog. Just a few days after this incident, Moses and Aaron went again to Pharaoh and asked him, 'O Pharaoh! Let my people go to serve their God. If you refuse to let them go, then God will send a curse of frogs over all your territory. The Nile will teem with frogs. They will come up and enter into your palace and into your bedroom and onto your bed, into the houses of your servants, too, and among your people, even into your utensils items and your kneading bowls. The frogs will come up over you and your people and all your servants.'

After that, Moses and Aaron left Pharaoh's presence and went upon the River Nile. There Aaron stretched out his hand over the waters of the Nile, and in return, the frogs came up and covered the land of Egypt. No empty land but frogs filled Egypt.

The people again presented on the throne of Pharaoh. They said to Pharaoh that Moses and Aaron have made frogs overrun the land of Egypt. This has ruined our lives and castles. Let us get rid of this trouble.

Pharaoh summoned Moses and Aaron and said, 'Moses! Pray to your God to remove the frogs from me and my people, and I will let the people go to sacrifice to God this time.'

Moses answered Pharaoh, 'Please, designate for me the time when I am to pray for you and your servants and your people, to get rid of the frogs from you and your houses.'

'Tomorrow,' he said.

Then Moses replied, 'It will be as you have said, so that you may know that there is none like the God. The frogs will leave you and your houses, your servants and your people; they will be left only in the Nile.'

Moses and Aaron left Pharaoh's presence, Aaron cried out

to God on account of the frogs that he had inflicted on Pharaoh. The frogs left the houses, the courtyards, and went from the fields. When this curse had also gone from Egypt after Aaron's prayer, Amun in the court of Pharaoh said, 'We have fully determined that no doubt, Moses is the greatest magician. He is causing trouble in Egypt on basis of his great magic. Is anyone here in Egypt who can confront this stiff magician?'

When Pharaoh saw this respite, he became obstinate and did not listen to them again.

IV Curse – The Gnats. When Pharaoh did not listen to Moses and Aaron this time also, then just after three days, Moses stretched out his Asa and struck the dust on the earth in the desert, and gnats came upon human beings and beasts alike. All the dust of the desert turned into gnats throughout the land of Egypt. The gnats were on human beings and beasts alike. It was a disaster that was taking both skin and flesh from people's bodies. Then the magicians said to Pharaoh, 'This is the finger of God.' Yet Pharaoh hardened his heart and would not listen to them. And once more Pharaoh became obstinate and would not let the people of Bani Israel go.

V Curse – Pestilence. When Pharaoh did not take notice of Moses then God struck the livestock in the field, horses, donkeys, camels, herds, and flocks – with a very severe pestilence. This time also God distinguished between the livestock of Bani Israel in Egypt so that nothing belonging to Bani Israel died. Pharaoh also found upon inquiry that not even one of the livestock of the Bani Israel had died.

VI Curse – The Boils. Just after a few days of this incident, Moses and Aaron went to Pharaoh's court and asked him, 'O Pharaoh! Let my people go to serve their God. If you refuse to let them go, then God will send a curse of boils on you and your kingdom.' Haman and Amun this time also made fun of Moses and Aaron and both were thrown out of the palace.

So, Moses took the soot from a kiln and scattered it toward the sky. It turned into fine dust over the whole land of Egypt and caused festering boils on human beings and beasts alike throughout the land of Egypt. But God hardened Pharaoh's heart, and he took no notice of them.

VII Curse – Water Turned to Blood. Pharaoh and the Egyptians as well turned away and did not care for Moses' explanations. Then, on a day when Pharaoh was there on the bank of River Nile, a terrible curse came over Egypt. This curse was so tough that never before had such a dreaded curse come upon him.

What Moses and Aaron did, exactly, was that Moses raised his Asa and struck the waters in the Nile in full view of Pharaoh and his servants on the opposite bank of the River Nile, and all the water in the Nile was changed into blood. There was blood throughout the land of Egypt. All kinds of water turned into blood for all Egyptians. The water of the River Nile turned all red. An Egyptian would take whatever clean water he could in his hand, it would turn into blood. The fish in the Nile all died.

For Bani Israel, all kinds of water was completely neat and clean.

When many days passed in this condition, people started dying due to thirst. The situation was similar in the palace of the Pharaoh themselves. Even Pharaoh, when he put his hand on the water vessel, his water would become blood. Pharaoh had no water himself for three days. His lips had dried up with thirst. His condition was such that as soon as a pot of water was brought in front of him, that water vessel was immediately changed into blood.

In these worst situations, some women from Egypt went to the houses of Bani Israel and requested water. There, seeing the abnormal condition, when the woman of Bani Israel poured water into the hands of that Egyptian woman from her pot, the clean water turned into blood before falling into her hand.

Seeing this, an Egyptian woman started crying and got down there. When many more days passed in this condition and there was no hope left from the Pharaoh, then these people of Egypt again appeared in Moses' service. On reaching in front of Moses and Aaron, one of them spoke with the severity of thirst and dry lips.

'Moses, this time we are surrounded by a very tough curse. Our women and children are dying of thirst. We see that you are kind and compassionate. You should show your mercy to our previous disobedience to us and our children so that we can follow the path shown by you. This time we are scared of this terrible disaster. If you avoid this huge trouble from us this time, then we will bring true faith to your God.'

On hearing the condition of these people, Moses went with those Egyptians to the River Nile and saw the amazing condition with their eyes.

On assurance of the Egyptians, Moses lifted both his hands upwards toward the sky. Shortly, there, that red blood flowing away in the River Nile changed from one side into clean water. Seeing this happy sight, those Egyptians broke down over the water and did not take care of the promise made to Moses.

When they had all drank water, Moses reminded them of their call. Then a man among them turned his eyes and said, 'O Moses! This time, you give us some time that after consulting with our family, we will again appear before you to consider and worry about your words.' And they returned from there.

This time also Moses and Aaron kept watching these haters and evils go away. As Moses explained to them and wanted their care, the result was nothing but failure, and they progressed in evil and disobedience. Pharaoh as well as the Egyptians took no notice of Moses and Aaron after this much effort.

VIII Curse – the Darkness. When Egyptians, as well as Pharaoh, took no notice of them, one day in the wilderness Moses stretched out his hand toward the sky, immediately, there was dense darkness throughout the land of Egypt. People could not see one another nor could they get up from where they were, for three days. But all the Israelites had light where they lived.

Pharaoh then summoned Moses and Aaron and said, 'O Moses! Go, serve your God. Only your flocks and herds will be detained. Even your little ones may go with you.'

Moses replied, 'You also must give us sacrifices and burnt offerings to make to God. Our livestock also must go with us. Not an animal must be left behind, for some of them, we will select for service to the God; but we will not know with which ones we are to serve until we reach there.'

Pharaoh said to Moses in great anger, 'Leave me, and see to it that you do not see my face again! For the day you do see my face, you will die!'

Moses replied, 'You are right! I will never see your face again till you die.' Moses and Aaron left the court forever.

Amun came forward and urged Pharaoh! 'O great Pharaoh! Moses is a very big magician, and you have no alternative in magic against him. On his emphasis, he is cursing your kingdom in so many ways, and Moses is now out of your control.

'Both brothers are ruining and destroying your religion. Moses' fire has now reached your palace. If you have to do something, then in order to stop the way the religion of Moses is getting to succeed, Moses should be defamed in the eyes of the people.

'Or Moses should be lured with gold and silver, and in this work, the Karoon can give us some way to achieve our objective or show some other way.'

Karoon was summoned to the court of Pharaoh.

Treasure of Karoon

Karoon was a malicious and beautiful man from Bani Israel itself. While living in Egypt, he had a strange literatus. He had Alchemia knowledge also.

He was engaged in the experiments day and night on the basis of Alchemia. With these strange experiments, he had piled up the gold in Egypt. He used to provide a huge quantity of gold to Pharaoh. That's why this Kingdom of Pharaoh was also known as the 'Empire of Gold'.

Karoon was a business-minded person and weak in reliance. For him, wealth was everything. He used to spend his wealth to cover his own timidity. For this, he also built a large palace, which was decorated with gold and diamonds and jewels, his camels, horses, and horsemen were decorated with diamonds, jewels, and gold ornaments. Within this palace, he had founded his laboratory on one side for experiments.

There was a large group of artisans in that laboratory working day and night in the fiery furnaces, passing various kinds of minerals and metals from various types of alchemy processes to continue to extract gold. Karoon himself would be engaged in the production of gold on top of all this.

When he used to go out on the ride, a great convoy would accompany him and a large group of people would stand on either side of the road to see him. People would look at the pride and regards of Karun and say, 'How fortunate is the Karoon. Hopefully! We too get as much as the Karoon has got.'

One day when Moses and Aaron said to him that God has

given you so much wealth that forty camels carry only the keys of your treasuries, then spend one of the thousand on the way of God, but the Karoon found these expenses difficult and said, 'I have earned this wealth through my knowledge and hard work. People should go and earn by doing hard work. I do not stop anyone from working hard.'

He had also taken many Bani Israel with him and said to them, 'You people are very foolish, and do not understand anything. All of you obey Moses, while his motive is that whatever little or more you have, to take from you in the name of God and leave you poor. You are the one who does not understand and does not question him.'

Then one day, when Karoon was summoned to the court of the Pharaoh, Karoon appeared in the court of the Pharaoh.

Amun! 'O Karoon! Your brothers, Moses and Aaron, roam throughout this country, spoiling the religion of the great Pharaoh.

'Well, have you any firm arrangement to prevent the fire of Moses and his religion? Moses is turning the hearts of people with the help of his magic. We consider you to be our well-wisher.'

Karoon (turning to Pharaoh)! 'O great Pharaoh! Moses is turning the hearts of people by his magic. So, why don't we put such blame on Moses that the hearts of the people go away from him and then they also turn from his religion.'

In this way, Karoon summoned an ill-fated woman to him, and lured her with a lot of goods and loyalty, and said that in front of all the people, when Moses was present there, she should have to make blame over Moses that he had done bad work with her.

Moses used to give people righteous advice from time to time, people would gather to listen to recitation. One day, when

Moses was explaining to the people, Karoon with his grace and pride and a few non-believers like him, arrived at the recitation of Moses. They were like Karoon, a crowd of ill-fated, brought with him there in which that raffish woman also came and sat quietly in a side of the assembly. For the Karoon, a majestic throne was set up in the assembly on which he started laughing and mocking his people. Moses was sitting on a stone in a high place, and he was reciting the accumulated assembly.

'Brothers! Forever peace and well-being are for him who does not turn his back on the grace of the God who made the land and the sky and everything in between these two, and it has not been difficult to make it. He created every living thing, then gave them perceptibility of every good and bad path. All who live have to taste death. Everyone has to return to Him one day, then worship of Him is right on you. And the person who turns his face on it, becomes one of the losers. He is the only one who can turn hearts.'

In this way, when this recitation became warm and the impulse of knowledge and reality started beating in Moses' chest, then that woman stood up and put an allegation on Moses. When that woman got up to say something, she could not speak. Her voice stopped. When the eyes of all the people woke up to that woman, Karun saw that the woman was trying hard to say something, but despite applying her full strength, she could not speak even a word, then she became very disappointed.

When Moses saw that a woman stood on one side of the assembly and wanted to say something but was unable to speak, Moses said, 'O my sister! I, Moses, Prophet of God command you, to tell whatever you want to say.'

Upon hearing these words of Moses, that woman began to weep and her tongue opened, so bid,

'O Bani Israel! this Karoon is an enemy of the true Moses. Yesterday, he called me in his palace and honored me with a lot of wealth and said that I should blame the true Moses in the common assembly and say that Moses had done a bad job with me. But I bear witness that Moses is the true prophet of his Lord. And I avoid my past evils right now.'

Hearing this woman's statement, Bani Israel was shocked and began to rave at Karoon. Moses got angry and he stood up and raised his hands toward the sky and said, 'O Jehovah! This enemy of yours intended to hurt me and wanted to discredit me.'

Now Moses began to tremble in anger and fingered toward Karoon.

'O Bani Israel! As my Lord made me superior over Pharaoh, the same he has sent on Karoon, whoever is a denier like him, he should stay with him and whoever is firm with his Lord, should get away from him.' Seeing the raging anger of Moses, all the people who were with him quickly shied away from him.

Seeing this, Karoon stood up from his throne and started to mourn the people who came with him. Moses became more furious and pointed his right-hand finger toward Karun and said, 'O land! Get hold of him!'

The ground caught Karoon up to his ankles there.

Karoon laughed and said, 'O Moses! What magic is this?'

Moses began to tremble with anger. He ordered the land – 'O land! hold him!'

Karoon got stuck to his knees on the ground. Now Karoon got nervous. Moses again ordered,

'O land! hold him!'

Karoon went into half the ground. Now the Karoon shouted, 'O Moses! Save me!'

Moses again ordered the ground, 'Hold him!'

Karoon got sunk up to the neck and started praying, 'Moses! Forgive me, Moses forgive me.'

Moses again ordered the land, 'Take hold of him!'

Now Karoon got completely trapped in the ground. And there became a dark blind eyelet there, and those people who aspired to his status yesterday started saying,

'He is ill-fated! God himself spreads livelihood for whom he wants and tightens for whom he wishes. Our fate was not like Karoon, otherwise, we would have been trapped in the ground.'

Hearing this, a person who used to live with Karoon said, 'Moses lured Karoon into the ground with the help of his stiff magic to acquire the treasures and palaces of Karoon.'

When this thing came to the ears of Moses, Moses immediately in a loud voice ordered the land 'All the treasures, jewels, palaces, and all the gold and silver should be immersed in the ground in a way no one can get anything from it.'

As soon as Moses had said this, the whole great palace of the Karoon, afar in Egypt, and his large gold and silver storage house began to sink into the sand, like all of them were placed on the sand on water and suddenly started getting trapped in the earth.

In a few moments, where the high palace of the Karoon and the treasures of gold and silver were present, there was now a level plain of sand, and particles of gold and silver were visible in that sand from far and wide. In this way, the treasure of Karoon whose keys once used to carry a group of camels, today that treasure disappeared somewhere inside a balloon of dust and was mixed in the sand in such a way that none of the human beings had anything from it.

When Ankhenamesh disappeared from the castle of Pharaoh through the strange shape of a flower on the floor, he reached into the forest and sat on a mountain. Soldiers, sent by Haman, arrived in the forest, looking for him, and saw that Ankhenamesh was sitting on a rock with his face facing the sun, on top of the cliff and closing his eyes. At the same distance, four terrible wolves were also guarding him with legs spread out and alert.

Now as soon as those soldiers made their move toward Ankhenamesh, those dreaded wolves, who were still looking in a particular direction, when they noticed the movement of soldiers of Haman, they stood up their ears. The feet of that small Army stopped in an instant. And when the fiery red wolf's burning red eyes went toward those soldiers, that Army was in a great panic. Seeing this incident, all the soldiers were scared and ran back. After going to Egypt, the whole story was told to Haman. Ankhenamesh is sitting there alone in a dangerous bayonet. And very dangerous wolves are guarding him around. It is difficult for us to overcome it, and there is a big risk in reaching it.

Haman said, 'Shut up foolish and beware not to take such a thing out in front of anyone else. The religion of Moses will be advanced by these things, and I warn you that no one else is aware of this matter. In the royal court, you must say that Ankhenamesh has moved into the deep forest or wolves have eaten him.

Walking with God

Haman! 'O Pharaoh! Will you allow Moses and Bani Israel to be freed in order to spoil your oppressed in your kingdom and to deny you creating trouble in your kingdom? Or should Moses and Bani Israel be slaughtered so that no one remains to take the name of another God than you?'

Pharaoh! 'O, my courtiers! Well, what is your opinion about this! I saw no other God than me for you.'

A courtier came forward and said, 'O great Pharaoh! surround the Bani Israel and slaughter their men and keep the women alive for their sake... If you have to do it, then do it.'

Amun (from their place)! 'O Pharaoh! It is not so easy to do what your courtiers described now. Haven't you seen, how the strange stick that Moses has, how outlandish it is. It will not be easy for you to control him. If you have to do it, then do this, a royal food-cloth, which takes place in your palace, both morning and evening, this is increasing the burden on the treasury however long the conflict continues with Moses, then you issue such a command. On this royal food-cloth of the Pharaoh, only they should come for food who have accepted Pharaoh as their only God.' So, everyone liked the idea of Amun. Therefore, the order was issued, only those were included on royal food-cloth who showed their belief to the great Pharaoh.

Even after Bani Israel refused to eat at the food-cloth of Pharaoh, as well refused to accept Pharaoh as their God, there was a growing intervening of Moses and Aaron within the community of Egypt. Only after a few days, from the testimonies of their courtiers, Pharaoh made it clear that the boys of Bani Israel should be slaughtered, and the girls should be allowed to stay alive.

Bani Israel came in a big panic. The oppression which broke on Bani Israel this time was very terrible and frightening. So, all the people of Bani Israel gathered in one place and decided to plead with Moses. When all of them came to Moses, Moses was sitting on a stone, so the people of Israel came crying to Moses and said, 'O Moses! We and our community are devastated. Pharaoh has destroyed us. Our children have been snatched from their mother's arms and are being murdered.'

Another person pleaded (crying)! 'Moses! When you were not born, even at that time, Pharaoh had snatched away thousands of our children from the arms of mothers and while you were with us, we still had a lot of persecution. Now we do not have the strength to be patient.'

Another old man of Bani Israel came forward crying, bowing down, and taking help of sticks! 'O Moses! Our father and grandfather had given us the notice of your arrival and redemption from these troubles. When you got down to the Madaian, Pharaoh deployed us into stiff eventuation's. We continued to tolerate all these sufferings that one day you will come, and we will get rid of these stiff evaluations. But since you have come, we see that our misery and sorrow have increased more. Our chests are riddled, our innocent children are snatched from us, we have no more patience. If you dictate, then we should depart from this land.'

Hearing these circumstances, Moses wept and assured the people and said, 'O my community! The day is not far when your enemy will be assassinated and your Lord will make you owner for this country, because he sees your condition and will spare you soon from this oppression because the scale of Pharaoh's oppression is full. The day of promise for the exterminating of Egypt and Pharaoh has come closer.'

Saying this, Moses withdrew from there and took the path to the deep forest. On reaching the foothills of a mountain, he fell to the ground and started praying to his Lord! 'O Jehovah! Help my community. Rescue them from the hands of the bloodthirsty Pharaoh. The more I explain to him, the more he is becoming undutiful. My community is heavily tempted. You must no more examine them and get rid of the oppressor.'

Then Jehovah's word sounded. 'O Moses! The scale of the oppression of Pharaoh and his followers is full. The relaxation he had to get, he has got. He remains cruel and drastic. One more plague, I will bring upon Pharaoh and upon Egypt. Instruct the people that every man is to ask his neighbor, and every woman her neighbor, for silver and gold articles and for clothing. About midnight, I will go forth through Egypt. Every firstborn in the land of Egypt will die, from the firstborn of Pharaoh who sits on his throne to the firstborn of the slave-girl as well as all the firstborn of the animals. Then there will be loud wailing throughout the land of Egypt. But among all the Bani Israel, among human beings and animals alike, not even a dog will growl, so that you may know that the God distinguishes between Egypt and Bani Israel. All these servants of yours will then come down to me and bow down before me.

'In the land of Egypt, this month will stand at the head of your calendar; you will reckon it the first month of the year. Tell the whole community of Bani Israel, on the tenth of this month, every family must procure for itself a lamb, one apiece for each household. If a household is too small for a lamb, it along with its nearest neighbor will procure one. Your lamb must be a year-old male and without blemish. You may take it from either the sheep or the goats. You will keep it until the fourteenth day of this month, and then, with the whole community of Israel assembled, it will be slaughtered during the evening twilight. They will take some of its blood and apply it to the two doorposts and the lintel of the houses in which they eat it. They will consume its meat that same night, eating it roasted. Do not eat any of it raw or even boiled in water, but roasted, with its head and shanks and inner organs. You must not keep any of it beyond the morning; whatever is leftover in the morning must be burned up.

'For on this same night, death will go through Egypt, striking down every firstborn in the land, human beings and beasts alike, and executing judgment on all Egypt. But for you, the blood will be the mark of the houses where you live. Seeing the blood, death will pass over you; thereby, no destructive blow will come upon you.

'You will dedicate to Jehovah every firstborn that opens the womb, and every firstborn male of your animals will belong to Jehovah. Every firstborn of a donkey you will ransom with a sheep. If you do not ransom it, you will break its neck. Every human firstborn of your sons you must ransom with a sheep or a goat. And when your son asks you later on, "What does this mean?" you will tell him, "With a strong hand, Jehovah brought us out of Egypt, out of a house of slavery. When Pharaoh stubbornly refused to let us go, Jehovah killed every firstborn in the land of Egypt, the firstborn of human beings and beasts alike. That is why, I sacrifice to Jehovah every male that opens the womb, and why I ransom every firstborn of my sons." It will be like a sign on your hand and a band on your forehead that with a strong hand Jehovah brought us out of Egypt.'

Moses returned from there, and when he reached the middle of Bani Israel, he stood on a high place, and declared,

'Every man present here should inform all that are not. The God of your forefathers Abraham, Isaac and Yaqub (Jacob) command you, this month is to be for you the first month, the first month of your year for Bani Israel that on the tenth day of this month each man is to take a lamb for his family, one for each household. If any household is too small for a whole lamb, they must share one with their nearest neighbor, having taken into account the number of people there are. You are to determine the amount of lamb needed in accordance with what each person will eat.

'The animals you choose must be year-old males without any defect, and you may take them from the sheep or the goats.

'Take care of them until the fourteenth day of the month, when all the members of the community of Bani Israel must slaughter them at twilight.

'Then they are to take some of the blood and put it on the sides and tops of the doorframes of the houses where they eat the lambs.

'That same night, they are to eat the meat roasted over the fire, along with bitter herbs, and bread made without yeast.

'Do not eat the meat raw or boiled in water, but roast it over a fire.

'Do not leave any of it till morning; if some is left till morning, you must burn it.

'No foreigner may eat it. Any slave you have bought may eat it after you have circumcised him, but a temporary resident or a hired worker may not eat it. The same law applies both to the native-born and to the foreigner residing among you.

'For seven days you are to eat bread made without yeast. On

the first day remove the yeast from your houses, for whoever eats anything with yeast in it from the first day through the seventh must be cut off from Israel.

'On the first day, hold a sacred assembly and another one on the seventh day. Do no work at all on these days, except to prepare food for everyone to eat; that is all you may do.

'Celebrate the Festival of Unleavened Bread, because it was on this very day that I brought your divisions out of Egypt. Celebrate this day as a lasting ordinance for the generations to come.

'In the first month, you are to eat bread made without yeast, from the evening of the fourteenth day until the evening of the twenty-first day.

'For seven days, no yeast is to be found in your houses. And anyone, whether foreigner or native-born, who eats anything with yeast in it must be cut off from the Bani Israel.

'Eat nothing made with yeast. Wherever you live, you must eat unleavened bread.'

Then Moses summoned all the elders of Israel and said to them, 'Go at once and select the animals for your families and slaughter the Passover lamb.

'Take a bunch of plant leaves, dip it into the blood in the basin, and put some of the blood on both sides of the doorframe. None of you shall go out of this door of your house until morning.

'When the death goes through the land to strike down the Egyptians, it will see the blood on the doorframe and will not enter your houses and strike your house.

'When you enter the land that God will give you as he promised, observe this ceremony.

'And when your children ask you, "What does this ceremony mean to you?" then tell them, "It is the Passover sacrifice to the

God, who passed over the houses of Bani Israel in Egypt and spared our homes when he struck down the Egyptians.'" Then Bani Israel bowed down and worshiped.

Moses ordered Bani Israel to finally set out from Ramesses for Succoth, about six hundred thousand men on foot, not counting the children. A crowd of mixed ancestry also went up with them, with livestock in great abundance, both flocks and herds. The time Bani Israel had stayed in Egypt was four hundred and thirty years. At the end of four hundred and thirty years, on this very date, all the armies of the Bani Israel left the land of Egypt.

During this Exodus, Moses explained to Bani Israel the Passover enactment. All Bani Israel did exactly as Moses and Aaron commanded them. On that same day, Moses brought Bani Israel out of the land of Egypt.

Now as the evening was settling down, the cold was also increasing. It was forbidden to light a fire on this ground. Now in the middle of the night, when the winter was in full swing, Moses stood in a high place and did this title to all Bani Israel.

Moses said to the people, 'Jehovah has done you a great favor that you have been spared from the hands of the bloodthirsty. Remember, this day on which you came out of Egypt, out of a house of slavery. For it was with a strong hand that Jehovah brought you out from there. Nothing made with leaven may be eaten. This day on which you are going out is in the month of Abib. For seven days, you will eat unleavened bread, and the seventh day will also be a festival. Unleavened bread may be eaten during the seven days, but nothing leavened and no leaven may be found in your possession in all your territory.

'So, I command you to depart, it is not strange that your Lord gives you a better place than it, so follow me and do not look back. Your Lord will give you a country where there will be rivers of milk and honey.' Moses and Aaron proceeded through the forest path along with Bani Israel.

While walking, there was a bit of a misunderstanding, so all the Army stopped. There was darkness all around. Then Aaron said to Moses, 'This seems to be the way that we had gone a little while ago.'

'Then what is the reason that we forget the way even though this path is familiar to us.'

All were wondering with surprise then a greybeard of Bani Israel came forward and said, 'I understand. A very important thing has remained. That is, your great grandfather Hazrat Yusuf had taught his children during his reign and took pity that when the Bani Israelis came out of Egypt, that they took his coffin with him. This is the only reason that we forget the way.'

Moses gave a voice in Battalion – 'Is there anyone who knows the place of Hazrat Yusuf's tomb?'

Then an old woman from Battalion came forward and said, 'I know the site of the tomb of Hazrat Yusuf. But I won't tell it for free.'

Moses said, 'What is your purpose in this?'

The old lady said, 'Take me on your ride back to Egypt. From this, my purpose is that I should also be called Moses Companion.'

Moses took the old woman on his ride, took some other people along, and turned to Egypt. Reaching the banks of the great River Nile in Egypt, the old woman revealed the trail of Yusuf's tomb in a wave of the great Nile, that was illuminated even in the dark. Our comrades who came with Moses took the coffin of Hazrat Yusuf out of the river. When Hazrat Yusuf's coffin was brought out of the river, a pillar of white light became visible in front of Hazrat Yusuf's coffin. When Moses went to the Battalion with the coffin, the lighted column also went ahead. In this way, Moses brought the coffin of Hazrat Yusuf to Batallion. With the arrival of the coffin of Hazrat Yusuf, the missing path to the Battalion was now clear and that pillar of white light also went ahead of the Battalion. Moses was moving forward with a fear equally in the heart that Pharaoh should not come back from behind with their unfortunate divine Army.

IX Curse – The Death of the Firstborn. When Moses was out of the borders of Ramesses with Bani Israel, then in the same night every firstborn in the land of Egypt died, from the firstborn of Pharaoh who sits on his throne to the firstborn of the slave-girl who is at the hand mill, as well as all the firstborn of the animals. There was a loud wailing throughout the land of Egypt, such as had never been, nor will ever be again. When it happened, the Egyptians ran toward the Pharaoh's court.

They urged in Pharaoh's court in the presence of Haman and Amun (bitterly wept), 'O Pharaoh, Moses on the basis of his stiff magic, has made great damage this time in every house in your kingdom. There is at least one death from among humans to animals throughout your kingdom, none of the Bani Israel is in their houses and neighborhoods. All the houses are empty and deserted, we suspect that Moses has left Egypt with Bani Israel after ruining your country. Will you leave him casually on his dare?'

Haman, Amun, and all the other courtiers present in the court were shocked. Pharaoh, who was sitting alone on his throne, stood up, and said, 'I allowed Moses and Bani Israel to leave my kingdom, now he has breached my mercy and should not dare. Now he will see my anger.

Pharaoh invoked the divine army of Ahmose in furious anger.

'Abadzu Mateen Amket Ah Ma to Ahmose.'

Then the divine army of Ahmose queued outside the palace of Pharaoh with a shield and a golden spear in hand. On the other hand, Pharaoh took thousands of good chariots and placed all the warriors on them. The horsemen rode on their two-wheeled chariots and traveled outside the palace with Haman and other strength. Pharaoh himself had a divine golden spear in one hand and a chariot filled with quivers and arrows. In this way, another six hundred fighters came to rest in front of the Army of Pharaoh, Haman, and Ahmose with chariots. When looking back you could see a heavy Army standing behind, as far as could be seen. When they all were waiting for the order for the left then a black cloud was seen in the sky.

X Curse – The Hail. When that black cloud became close to them, a loud thunderous sound was heard inside it. When the Pharaoh looked toward it, the clouds started to make a thundering sound along with fierce hail. Hail and lightning was flashing here and there through the hail. The hailstones that fell on the ground were mixed with fire and these hailstones were so large that since the time the country of Egypt was settled, such hail had never fallen in Egypt. When this fiery hail started raining on Pharaoh and his divine Army, the hail started destroying the Army. Now this hail started destroying the houses, palaces, fields, and produce of Egypt.

All the trees in the field broke down and started burning. On the other hand, the palace of Pharaoh caught fire. When the hail of fire fell on the palace, the bastions of the palace would collapse and disintegrate far and wide. In this way, the palaces of Pharaoh were ruined and ruined before the eyes of Pharaoh.

Then Haman filled with anger and shouted, 'Move fast or else all of you will be destroyed and ruined here by this heavy magic of Moses. Seeing all this, Pharaoh became hardened and, in a state of great anger, ordered the Army to march away and flee with the power and take Moses and Bani Israel at the tip of the spears.

This dreaded Army of Pharaoh was running away blowing dust and mud with innumerable chariot riders and the army of Ahmose, who were running very fast behind, was creating great panic in the hearts of the watchers.

On the other hand, Moses and Aaron with Bani Israel were heading forward fast in the bitter cold covering their faces and tightening their scarf. Bani Israel were trying to turn their faces away from biting cold.

The Army was moving fast so that the flames of fire falling from the sky blocked the path of this great Army. Pharaoh and Haman stopped seeing the balloon rising from this fire.

Pharaoh pointed his hand to all the warriors riding their chariots, immediately the spears of all warriors were opened by knocking, and everyone flew their open spears into the sky. These spears rose up in the sky and joined the circle of ten-ten and started moving in the clouds above, and then the surrounding clouds were drawn inside. These circles pulled the surrounding clouds and gathered them at a point at which lightning started to crack.

And clouds started pouring heavy water from the sky and when the water started to fall on top of the fire, it started extinguishing the storm on the way. Haman was very nervous to see this disaster falling from the sky, but Haman now looked satisfied after seeing the feats of Pharaoh. Now this storm of water, raining from the sky, had silenced the wall of fire standing in the middle of the Army, then Pharaoh and Haman commanded the Army to proceed with great vigor.

Moses and Aaron were leading Bani Israel with fast steps. In this row, they have seen the Darya-e-Kuljum (Red Sea) right in front of the eyes. Seeing the Darya-e-Kuljum (Red Sea) right in front of the eyes, which was flowing in full swing that day, Moses and Aaron became absolutely lifeless, as Moses and Aaron had been approaching a dry way with Bani Israel, but luck had brought them to the edge of the Darya-e-Kuljum (Red Sea).

Seeing Darya-e-Kuljum (Red Sea) in front of their eyes, the Israelites also got troubled.

In this situation, the people camped there, because the winter was also in great swing. Bani Israel made camp and started making fires. While Bani Israel were busy in all these activities, the great Army of Pharaoh was moving rapidly in pursuit. When Bani Israel saw the Army from the distance, they were horrified.

All came running toward the direction where Moses had stayed and said, 'O Moses! We are surrounded.'

Then another man said, 'O Moses! The Pharaoh surrounded us, did we not have tombs in Egypt, though you brought us here to die in the wilderness? Didn't we tell you in Egypt to let us stay there to service Egyptians; it was better for us to service Egyptians than to die in the wilderness.'

Moses said to the people, 'Don't be afraid, stand and see the salvation that Jehovah will do for you today. Because he has promised me to help. And his promise is true. And he sees us in every situation. You will never see the Egyptians, whom you see today. The Lord will fight for you today. So, you just look.'

Saying this, Moses turned away and went aside and raised his hands in prayer. 'O our adherent! My community is surrounded. It also has children, and weak, and women too. All are unarmed, they are unable to compete with the enemy, then you help them so that all these will glorify you and know you.'

Then the Lord gave voice to Moses, 'Moses! Why are you crying out to me? Command Bani Israel to depart. The one that is in your hand, hit it on the sea, so that the sea will give you the way.'

Moses turned to the community and said, 'O community! Jehovah has made it easy for you, let's move forward that the sea will give you a way!'

Aaron and the people of the community followed Moses. But some people were still looking at the sea with open mouths.

The Army of the Pharaoh and Haman, that was chasing fast, suddenly saw from the sky that a dense fog came between the Army of Pharaoh and Bani Israel. Pharaoh, Amun and Haman were confident that they would take Bani Israel and Moses soon on the tip of these divine spears. Suddenly, the fog became so dense that they all were forced and helpless to move forward. The darkness had become so much that nothing was visible to anyone.

Haman was still saying, 'Moses is a very big wizard. Even while running, he is performing such a heavy spell.'

Moses reached the bank of Darya-e-Kuljum (Red Sea). Standing there, for a while, he noticed the passion of flowing water in a full row of Darya-e-Kuljum (Red Sea). Moses raised his Asa in his hands and recited some spell and hit the water, In a very surprising way with a huge thunder, the water of the sea rose on both sides in the middle of Darya-e-Kuljum (Red Sea). The water stood upright on both sides and twelve broad paths were made in the middle of Darya-e-Kuljum (Red Sea).

When the sun also shone bright, Aaron said to the community, 'O Bani Israel! Glory your Lord for making his promise come true, start walking these strange paths to get rid of the enemy.'

When Aaron saw that there was fear in the community that if we entered it, the mountain of seawater, which is still standing straight, would fall on us, and we would be destroyed. Then Aaron came down the path with his family and then all the tribes also went on the paths between the sea. Seeing that which stood on both sides equal to the height of the mountain, their hearts scared them. The water seemed to rise up from the bottom on those steep walls.

On these unusual paths when Bani Israel moved forward fearfully one of them gently asked, 'O Moses! We are proceeding ahead with you on these strange paths, but we do not know whether the rest of our brothers are also running similarly or if they are trapped between these mountains like water walls, we are afraid of this.'

Moses was very angry on hearing this, but in an excusable degree to the community, raised his stick and struck it on these walls of water, then at the same time with great horror came a thunderous roar of water. Windows opened in the middle of the water walls, and every individual walking on the other side started looking completely clear. In this way, the twelve families of the twelve clans, with their sheep, goats, cows, and bulls, were moving forward looking at each other beneath the sea.

Now while the sun was shining exceedingly fast, the fog in which the Army of Pharaoh and Haman was trapped was slowly coming off.

Now Pharaoh and Haman, who were still lost in that fog, started to show a little bit to both of them. The Army again ran forward and reached the bank of the Red Sea. On reaching the bank, they observed that the community of Bani Israel that was present here some time ago was no longer there. When they glanced toward the Red Sea, they saw strange conditions which they had never seen. In the middle of the great Red Sea, there were twelve outlandish paths. Water was flowing on both sides of the paths vertically. The water was rising from the bottom with a heavy horror but was not falling on the way and the path looked absolutely dry. The water had risen up to the height of the mountain on both sides of the path. Seeing that, there was a great panic in the hearts of Pharaoh, Haman, Amun and the Army. The riders, who were riding the chariots standing behind, were watching this scenario with great surprise, and they were also afraid.

Pharaoh was frightened to see this heavy unusual scenario and said to Haman, 'O Haman! If Moses has crossed this great sea with the help of his heavy magic, then it is appropriate for us to return to Egypt and desist from pursuing Moses and Bani Israel.'

Haman (astonished)! 'It would be a matter of great shame on us if the Bani Israel crossed the sea by the magic of Moses and we returned empty-handed to Egypt so that the women of Egypt would laugh at us.'

Pharaoh (baffled)! 'So, what to do in such a situation?'

Destruction of Pharaoh

Haman! 'O great Pharaoh! Just as Moses has crossed Bani Israel through these strange paths, you should also put your Army on these paths so that we can soon get Moses and his people.'

In this way, Pharaoh put his chariot on the strange path in the Red Sea. From behind, all the Army also landed on those paths. When the entire Army landed in the Red Sea, on observing, the heart of the Army sat down watching the situation there.

A chariot rider said, 'Didn't you see that Pharaoh has such a supernatural power that today even the Red Sea has given him the path from amongst themselves. 'And did you not see that he had rained once even before.'

And in this way, Pharaoh's Army kept running fast forward. But they were very terrified after seeing the scenario there. The dry path in the middle, and the standing water as high as the mountain on both sides, which was rising up from the bottom with a huge thunder, there was also an abundance of perfect square windows in a way that one walking on one path was able to see other side walking easily.

Likewise, when Pharaoh, Haman, and all their armies reached the middle of the sea and its dry and dangerous paths, the chariot of Pharaoh stopped with a sharp jerk in the middle. Horses connected in the chariot stood together from the front, Pharaoh suddenly fell from his chariot to the front ahead of the horses on a stony path, the chariot overturned with a terrific sound, barely saving Pharaoh. The chariot of the Pharaoh broke into pieces. The wheels of the chariot got separated. His arrows and that golden spear also fell from the chariot and fell into one of those paths. When Haman saw that the chariot of Pharaoh had overturned and the Pharaoh had fallen, and the wheels of the chariots of Pharaoh had come out, he barely stopped his chariot. In the same row, the coming Army had stopped their chariots with their full strength. Despite that, so many chariots had hit the chariots ahead of him. In this way, the whole Army got stuck with each other. When they saw this strange scene of water, they got very nervous.

Fallen on stony paths, when Pharaoh tried to get up, he found a white-clothed stranger standing near his head.

Haman fearfully moved toward Pharaoh, seeing the strange water walls on both sides up to a large height. On reaching near Pharaoh, he was shocked to see Pharaoh from a distance as he conflicted with someone in anger, but there was no one against him. Haman observed from a distance,

Pharaoh! 'Who are you? Do you know the result of stopping our way?'

Pharaoh angrily used some power on him, but it did not affect him.

The stranger said very politely, 'There is an assignment between you and me, which is this.'

The stranger passes a royal assignment to Pharaoh. When he glanced at the royal assignment, he immediately remembered the assignment on that mountain in Egypt when he rained over his community. This stranger was present at the mouth of the cave.

So, Pharaoh simultaneously looked at the royal assignment which stated that,

'The punishment for a slave who opposes his rearing master and turns his face on him is that he should be immersed in Darya-

e-Kuljum.'

By signature – Pharaoh Ramesses

Now when the Pharaoh saw the face of the Divine spirit standing there, the color of the Pharaoh turned yellow.

On the other hand, Moses removed all his community Bani Israel across the sea and made sure that every one of the twelve clans had come across with his herds, then turned toward the Pharaoh, Haman, and his great Army. He saw the Army in the middle of the Red Sea. So, Moses stood up in a high place and got confirmation from all the Bani Israel that every man of each clan had crossed the sea. When it was clear, Moses reached the plinth of the Red Sea and hit his Asa (stick) on that straight standing water.

As soon as the Asa (stick) hit on straight standing water, the standing water started collapsing like a mountain. The mountain of water broke from the front and back on the Army of Pharaoh, and as soon as this surge of water grew on their side, the hearts of those who saw this were uprooted. What was happening to the water? The mountains were crumbling and falling heavily on the riders of Pharaoh and Haman. Now Pharaoh, Haman and his Army were surrounded by death on two sides. The water, which was carrying heavy devastation, arrived. When the Army was hit by the first shock of water, the Army flew away like a straw in the midst. The Army's chariots, horses attached to them and soldiers riding on them, were scattered in the raging water.

Haman shouted after seeing this terrible scene, 'Pharaoh! We are surrounded, our Army is getting destroyed. Save yourself and save us from drowning.'

The Pharaoh himself was very surprised and upset. He would sometimes see ahead of him and sometimes see the ruin behind. His eyes had spread. Death was running off toward him.

All the escape ways had been closed. Huge waves of water lifted the chariots and horses into the sky and were overturning them onto the Army standing ahead.

The Army was stuck on these strange routes in such a way that there was no way to escape. The surge of water was moving fast, swallowing the Army in the other eleven paths in the sea.

The Army's belongings started rising above in the sky by water and falling on the ridges and Haman himself. Haman screamed again, 'O Pharaoh! We are surrounded, is there a way to escape?'

This way, the water accumulated, it had conjoined.

Pharaoh now looked at the standing stranger, Pharaoh observed that he was looking at him with absolute peace and without any trouble.

The great destruction was on the head of Pharaoh. When he saw the mountain of water about to grab him, he got scared. As soon as he turned around looking at the assignment in his hands, that strange man disappeared from there!

Seeing the circumstances, Pharaoh was terrified and loudly shouted, 'I accept Moses.'

Pharaoh said that just at the moment, a water surge hit him and Haman and both were scattered in water shock. Pharaoh and Haman were surrounded by this storm of water and the deep water covered them. Seawater took Haman and took him away into the depths of the sea and hit his body on stones. There under the deep sea, the body of Haman was shattered by the divine spears of the Army of King Ahmose that were killing in a terrible way under the sea. Finally, a spear pierced Haman's body and sunk into a heavy stone lying in the depths of the sea, along with Haman's body.

Pharaoh was like a straw in the midst of life and death in

deep water, where death was the stuff all around. The bones of Pharaoh's body had now collided with the stones in the sea and had crushed inside his body. Meanwhile, the eyes of Pharaoh went onto the spears of Osiris who were coming toward him with lightning speed. In an instant, a spear passed through the Pharaoh's body, which caused the Pharaoh's body to be surrounded by dangerous electric waves. Pharaoh exerted his full force and pressed the divine spear with one hand, then the divine spear came out of his body and turned into a small golden instrument. The water of the sea all around became red with the blood of Pharaoh. The wandering celestial golden instrument was released from the hands of the Pharaoh and drowned in the depth of the sea.

The water of the Darya-e-Kuljum (Red Sea) had gathered for one purpose. That work was done. Pharaoh, Haman, and all his divine Army were drowned and destroyed.

So, when the storm of the Darya-e-Kuljum (Red Sea) was wreaked, Pharaoh, Haman, and their divine Army all garbled and overrun, yet Moses doubted that Pharaoh and Haman with their dreaded Army would come out of Darya-e-Kuljum (Red Sea) and take us on the point of our awesome spear.

Moses ordered Bani Israel to move fast along the edge of the Darya-e-Kuljum (Red Sea). In the same way, after walking for several days, Moses ordered Bani Israel to put up camp along the Darya-e-Kuljum (Red Sea), a place called Elim, where seventy date trees existed. This clump of date trees on the banks of Darya-e-Kuljum (Red Sea) and its surroundings was producing a very beautiful scenario on this place.

Some women of Bani Israel arrived on Darya-e-Kuljum (Red Sea). High waves were coming toward the shore from the sea with great enthusiasm. Then a huge wave of Darya-e –

Kuljum (Red Sea) brought a royal corpse to shore. Seeing this incident, the women got scared and left their water utensils, and ran toward the camp. Looking back from far away, there was a royal corpse lying on its face. Royal jewels and jams were present on the dead body. These women of Bani Israel went back to the camp and told Moses and Aaron all about how a royal corpse was lying on the banks of Darya-e-Kuljum. Immediately, Moses and Aaron reached the place on the edge of the sea with some people of the community and saw that there were many dead bodies scattered by the waves of the sea.

When one of them saw the corpse of the royal man lying face down, they suddenly got scared and lost their senses. The corpse was the Egyptian Pharaoh. The body was decorated with royal apex and symbols. Hands were empty, there was a gold necklace with a royal blue bead around the neck. There was sand on the mouth, which was probably filled inside the mouth. When Moses and Aaron went near, they recognized him, Moses was very inconsolable and said, 'O Pharaoh! I spent thirty years raising your house. Even, I have done my best to convince you. But you stood firm and turned your back and finally became the loser.' Then Moses ordered the clan headman to send the corpse of Pharaoh to Egypt, so that it would be a sign for the next generations.

A Congregation in the Wilderness

The whole congregation of the Israelites traveled from Elim and came out of Egypt, on the fifteenth day of the second month, to the wilderness called Sean, which is between Elim and Mount Sinai.

In the wilderness, all the congregation of the Israelites murmured against Moses and Aaron.

And the Israelites said to them, 'When we used to eat arbitrary food in the land of Egypt, sitting near the meat, then even if we were killed by the hand of the Lord, it was the best; but you have brought us into this forest to starve and kill all this society.'

Then the Lord said to Moses, 'Look, I will rain food for you from the sky; and these people will go out every day and gather daily food, that I will test them, whether they will follow my law or not. It will be that on the sixth day, they will have to be fed with food from those days, so prepare whatever they collect on that day.'

Then Moses and Aaron said to all the Israelites, 'In the evening, you will know that the one who has brought you out of the land of Egypt is the Lord.

'And in the morning, you will see the glory of the Lord because the Lord hears what you mumble. And what are we that you grumble at us?'

Then Moses said, 'This will happen when the Lord will allow you to eat meat and bread at dawn for dinner; because he listens to you who grumble at him. And what are we? Your grumbling is not on us but on Jehovah, it happens.'

Then Moses said to Aaron, 'Command the whole congregation of the Israelites to come before the Lord because he has heard their murmurings.'

And it came to pass that when Aaron was speaking to the whole congregation of the Israelites, they looked toward the wilderness, and saw the Lord in the bright cloud.

Then the Lord said to Moses,

'I have heard the murmurings of the Israelites; tell them that at sunset you will eat meat, and in the morning you will be satisfied with bread, and you will know that I am the Lord, your God.' Then it happened that in the evening quail came and sat on the whole camp; And in the morning, there was dew around the camp.

And when the dew has dried up, what do they see, that small peels are lying on the ground of the forest like the edges of the frost.

Seeing this, the Israelites, who did not know what it was, started saying among themselves that it is manna. Then Moses said to them, 'This is the food that the Lord gives you to eat.'

The command that the Lord has given is that you should make your food from it, that is, according to the number of your creatures, to gather one omer after each man. For those who are in the camp, they should share it for them only.

And the Israelites did the same, and some more and more.

When they measured it with omer, then the one who had more was left with nothing more, and the one who had little did not lack anything. Because each person had collected only enough for one person to eat.

Then Moses told them, 'No one should leave some of it till morning.'

Yet, they did not listen to Moses. Therefore, when some person left some of it for the morning, it got worms, and it started to settle. Then Moses became angry with them. They used to gather at dawn every day for their food, and when the sun was hot, it melted.

Then it happened that on the sixth day, they gathered two or two omers over the double, that is, per man, and all the heads of the congregation came and told Moses.

He said to them, 'It is the same thing that the Lord has said because tomorrow will be holy rest, that is, holy rest for the Lord; so cook what you have to cook in the oven, and what you want to cook, and so much of it. Leave what is left for the morning.'

When they left it till the morning, according to this command of Moses, neither did it settle nor did it get insects.

Then Moses said, 'Eat that today because today is the Sabbath of the Lord; therefore you will not find it in the field today.

'Six days, you will gather it; but the seventh day is a day of rest, it will not be found in it.'

Even then, some of the people went out to gather for the seventh day, but they could not find anything.

Then the Lord said to Moses, 'How long will you not keep my commandments and my law?

'See, the Lord has given you a day of rest, that is why he gives you two days of food on the sixth day; therefore, you should stay seated here, no one should go out of his place on the seventh day.'

So, people rested on the seventh day.

The House of Israel named the item manna; it was white like coriander and tasted like honey.

Then Moses said, 'The command that the Lord has given is

to leave one omer of it for your generation so that they will know what kind of bread the Lord used to bring us out of the land of Egypt into the wilderness.'

Then Moses said to Aaron, 'Take a vessel and fill one omer and place it in front of the Lord, that it may be kept for your generations.'

According to the command given by the Lord to Moses, Aaron placed it in front of the *ark of the witness*, that he might stay there.

The Israelites ate manna for forty years until they reached the inhabited country. They continued to eat manna until they reached the border of the land of Canaan.

Then the whole group of the Israelites went out of the wilderness called Sean, and traveled according to the Lord and set up their tents in Rephidim, and those people did not get drinking water there.

So, they argued with Moses and said, 'Give us drinking water.'

Moses said to them, 'Why do you argue with me? And why do you tempt the Lord?'

Then the people there thirsted for water, then they murmured at Moses, saying, 'Why have you brought us out of Egypt to kill us of thirst as well as our children and animals?'

Then Moses cried to the Lord.

The Lord said to Moses, 'Take some of the old men of Israel with you; and take the stick with which you struck on the Nile River, and move in front of the people. Hit a rock in Horeb mountain, then water will come out of it so that these people will drink.'

Then Moses did the same with the older people of Israel. And Moses named the place *Massa and Mareeba,* because the

Israelites debated there.

Then the Amalekites came and fought with the Israelites in Rephidim.

Then Moses said to Joshua, 'Sort out a number of men for us, and go out and fight with the Amalekites; and tomorrow I will stand on the top of the hill with the sticks of God in hand.' According to Moses' command, Joshua began to fight against the Amalekites; and Moses, Aaron, and Hur climbed to the top of the hill. And as long as Moses kept raising his hand, Israel prevailed; but whenever, he put her down, then Amalek prevailed.

And when Moses' hands were full, they took a stone and laid it under Moses, and he sat on it, and Aaron and Hur held their hands in one side; his hands held steady until sunset.

And Joshua defeated the Amalekites with the sword, with servants.

Then the Lord said to Moses, 'Write this thing in the book for remembrance and tell Joshua that I will completely erase the memory of Amalek from under the sky.'

Then Moses father-in-law Sueb brought Moses' wife, Siphora, who had previously been sent to her father's house, and her two sons. One of these was named Gershom by Moses, saying, 'I have been a foreigner in another country.'

And he named the other as Eliezer, 'The God of my father supported me and saved me with the sword of Pharaoh.' Moses' wife and sons, along with his father-in-law Sueb, came to Moses in the wilderness where he camped near God's mountain.

And he came and sent it to Moses saying, 'I am your father-in-law, and have brought your wife to you with both sons.' Then Moses went out to meet his father-in-law and worshiped and kissed him, and they came to the camp asking for mutual skills.

There Moses describes to his father-in-law what Jehovah has

done to Pharaoh, and the Egyptians for the Israelites, and what the Israelites have suffered along the way, then how Jehovah has been rescuing them.

The next day, Moses sat to judge the people, and from morning till evening, the people stood around Moses.

Seeing what Moses did for the people, his father-in-law said, 'What is this work that you do for the people? What is the reason that you are sitting alone, and the people are around you from morning to evening? Standing nearby?'

Moses said to his father-in-law, 'The reason is that people come to me to ask God.

'Whenever, they have a case, then they come to me, and I will do justice among them, and explain God's law and order to them.'

The father-in-law of Moses said to him, 'The work that you do is not good for you, but these people who are with you will surely get tired, because this work is too heavy for you; you cannot do it alone.

'Therefore, listen to me now, I give you advice, and God be with you. You go to God for these people, and you bring their cases to God.

'By revealing to them, the law and order, the path on which they should walk, and the work they have to do, they should have it explained to them. Be obedient, truthful, and hate the benefits of injustice; and appoint them chief over thousand-thousand, hundred-hundred, fifty-fifty, and ten-ten men.

And they should judge these people all the time; And bring all the big cases to you, and you should judge the small cases. Then your burden will be light, because they will also carry this burden with you. If you take this remedy, and God gives you such a command, then you will be able to stay, and all these people will be able to reach their place efficiently.'

Moses obeyed his father-in-law according to all his words.

Therefore, he chose virtuous men from all the Israelites, and made them chief over the thousand-thousand, hundred-hundred, fifty-fifty, ten-ten, people. And they began to judge all the people; They would have brought the case which was difficult to Moses, and they used to judge all the small cases themselves.

Then Moses sent his father-in-law away, and he took the path of his country.

On the same day that three months had passed since the Israelites had left Egypt, they traveled from Rephidim to the wilderness of Sinai. Then they encamped in the forest; there the Israelites camped in front of the mountain.

Then Moses climbed the mountain to God, and the Lord called him from the mountain and said, 'Say this to the Bani Israel and tell my word to the Israelites, "Have you seen what I did to the Egyptians? I have brought you on the eagle wings. So now, if you will obey me and obey my covenant, then out of all people, you will be my personal wealth. The whole earth is mine. And in my eyes, you will be a kingdom of priests and a holy nation." These are the things you have to say to the Israelites.'

When the third day came, the thunder clouds and lightning started shining at dawn, and there was blackening on the mountain, then the sound of the trumpet became very heavy, and all the people in the camp shivered. Then Moses took the people out of the camp to meet God; they stood under the mountain. When the sound of the trumpet grew and became very heavy, God called Moses to the top of the mountain, and said these words,

1. 'I am the Lord, your God, Who brought you out of the land of slavery, the land of Egypt.

2. 'You don't believe others as God. You shall not carve for yourself, an idol, nor a statue, which is in the heavens, or on the earth, or in the waters of the earth. You shall not worship them, nor worship them; I am God.
3. 'Remember, the sabbath to be considered holy. You work diligently for six days and do all your work, but the seventh day is a sabbath to the Lord, your God. Neither, do you do any other work in it, nor your son, nor your daughter, nor your slave, nor your maid, nor your animals, nor any foreigner who is inside your gates.
4. 'For in six days, the Lord made the heavens and the earth, and the sea, and all that is in them, and rested on the seventh day; For this reason, the Lord blessed the sabbath and made him holy.
5. 'Honor your father and your mother, so that you may live in the country your God Jehovah gives you for a long time.
6. 'You don't bleed.
7. 'You shall not commit adultery.
8. 'You must not steal.
9. 'Do not give false witness against anyone.
10. 'You shall not covet one's house; Neither greed of any women, nor of any slave-maid, or ox-donkey, nor of any thing of anyone.'

And all the people heard the roaring, and the words of the lightning and the trumpet, and the smoke rose, and they looked at the mountain, and, seeing, they shook and stood away; they said to Moses, 'You speak with us, then we will be able to hear; but God should not speak to us, lest we die.'

'These are the rules that you have to explain to them.

'When you buy a Hebrew slave, then he should serve for six

years, and in the seventh year, he should go and go free. If he has come alone, he will go alone; and if he has come with his wife, then his wife also leaves with him. If his Lord has given him a wife and has given birth to his son or daughters, then his wife and child should remain of that Lord, and he should leave alone.

'But if that slave says firmly, "I love my master, my wife, and my children; therefore, I will not go free." So, his master takes him to God. Then take him to the door or side of the door and pierce his ear with a string; Then he would always serve him.

'If someone sells his daughter to be a maid, he should not go out like a maid.

'If his master makes him his wife and is not happy with it, then let him be redeemed; After betraying him, he will not have the right to sell the hands of foreigners.

'If he has given her to his son, then treat him like a daughter.

'Even if, he takes another wife, he will not reduce his food, clothes, and company.

'And if she is reduced to these three things, then the woman will leave without paying any price. Whoever, kills a man so that he dies, he too must be killed.

'If he does not sit in his ambush, and it is at God's will that he falls into his hands, I will set a place for such a runner to run away.

'But if someone cruelly attacks someone and kills him with deceit, take him away from my altar to kill him.

'He who killed his father or mother must be put to death.

'Whoever steals a man, even if he is taken away and sold, if he is found near him, then he too must be killed.

'He who curses his father or mother must also be killed.

'If anyone hits his servant or maid with a stick so that he dies, then he must be punished. But if he survives two days, his master should not be punished because that slave is his wealth. If a man beats and maims a pregnant woman in such a way that she is miscarried, but there is no harm, then the punisher should be punished as much as the husband of that woman can with the consent of the punch.

'But if he does anything else, life instead of life.

'And eye to eye, and the tooth to tooth, and hand to hand, and foot to foot.

'And be punished the stain for the stain, and the wound for the wound. When someone hits his servant or maid's eye, so that it explodes, let him go free instead of his eye.

'And if he kills his servant or maid, and breaks his tooth, then he should let him go free instead of his tooth.

'If a bull hits a man or a woman so that it dies, the bull must surely be stoned to death, and its flesh is not eaten; but the master of the bull must be innocent. But if that bull has already had the habit of killing horns, and its master has not tied it even when it is expressed, and he kills a man or woman, then that bull should be stoned, and its owner to be killed.

'If the ransom is imposed on him, then whatever is prescribed for him to redeem his life will have to be given as much.

'Regardless of whether a bull has killed a son or a daughter, its master should be treated according to this rule. If the ox has killed a slave or a maid, the Lord of the bull should pay thirty shekels to the Lord of that slave, and the bull should be stoned.

'If a man opens a pit or dig it, and someone's ox or donkey falls into it, the one whose pit is, he should fill that loss; let the Lord of the animal buy it. If someone's bull hurts another bull so that it dies, then both of them sell the living bull and distribute it half by half; and share the carcass in the same way.

'If it is revealed that the bull had already had the habit of hitting the horn, but his master did not keep it tied, then surely he should fill the bull instead of the bull, but the carcass remains for the same.

'If someone grazes one's farm or vineyard with his animal, that is, leaving his animal so that he can graze the other field, then he should pay to the best of his vineyard.

'If a fire burns, and it bursts into thorns and burns a pile of flowers or a grain or a standing field, then the one who has lit the fire will surely compensate for the loss.

'If another person bequeaths a treasure of money or material, and it is stolen from his house, if the thief is caught, he will have to pay double.

'And if the thief is not caught, then the Lord of the house is brought to God to decide whether he has put his hand on the property of his brother.

'Whether the bull, the donkey, the sheep or the goat, whether the cloth or any kind of such lost thing, why should a crime be imposed? If two people say their respective cases, then both of them should come to God. And the one whom God blames, will fill the other with double.

'If someone hands over a donkey or ox or sheep or any other animal to keep, and he dies without being seen or is hurt, or looted.

'So, let the oath of Jehovah be given between them. "I have not put my hand on his wealth." Then the owner of the property believes it to be true, and the other will not have to fill it with anything. If it is truly stolen from him, let his master fill it.

'And if he is torn, he should bring the torn one for proof, then he will not have to fill it too.

'If anyone begs another animal, and if he is hurt by his

master, or if he dies, then he shall surely compensate him.

'If his master is with him, the other will not have to make up for his loss; and if he is a hirer, then his loss comes in his hire.

'If a man lures a girl whose marriage has not been talked about, then he liaises with her, then he will surely compensate and marry her. If her father absolutely refuses to give it to him, then the wearer should weigh the money according to the custom of the girls.

'Don't let the sorcerer survive.

'Whoever, commits an animal, must be killed.

'Whoever, sacrifices for any other deity except Jehovah should be annihilated.

'Do not persecute or alienate a foreigner, because you were also foreigners in the land of Egypt.

'Do not grieve any widow or orphaned child. If you give any kind of sorrow to such people, and they cry to me anything, I will surely listen to their cry. Then my anger will flare up, and I will get you killed by the sword, and your wives will become widows and your children orphans.

'If you give a loan of rupees to one of my people who lives with you, do not take the same interest from him as a Mahajan.

'If you ever take your brother's cloth tied, then return it before the sun sets, because it is his only garment, it will be the only garment of his body. Then how will he sleep without wearing it? And when he cries out to me, then I will listen to him, because I am pitiful.

'Do not curse God, nor curse the head of your people.

'Don't be late to give me some of your farm produce and fruit juice. Give me the firstborn of your sons.

'Likewise, give the firstborns of your cows and flocks. The child should be with his mother for seven days, and on the eighth day, you should give it to me. You are to be a holy man to me; for this reason, do not eat the flesh of the animal that is torn in the ground, throw it in front of the dogs.

'Do not spread falsehood. Do not stand with the wicked as an unjust witness.

'Do not follow many to do evil. Neither turn back after them and witness the spoiling of justice in the case; and do not do him any favor in the case of the pauper.

'If your enemy's bull or donkey finds you wandering, you must bring it back to him.

'Then if you see your enemy's donkey burdened, then even if you do not want your heart to be redeemed for its master, you must still support the master and get him rescued.

'Do not disturb justice in the trial of those who are poor among your people.

'Stay away from false trial, and do not slay the innocent and righteous, because I will not justify the wicked.

'Do not take a bribe, because a bribe also blinds the watchers, and reverses the words of the righteous.

'Do not darken a foreigner; you know the words of a foreigner's heart because you too were foreigners in the land of Egypt.

'Sow six years in your land and gather its produce; but in the seventh year, let it fall and leave it like that, then the poor people of your brothers should be able to eat from it, and whatever is left of them will be wild animals. Used in eating food. And do the same to your vineyards and olive groves. Do your work for six days, and rest on the seventh day; that your oxen and donkeys are slow, and your servants' sons and foreigners can cool themselves too. And be careful in what I have told you, and do not discuss the names of other Gods, but they should not even be heard from your mouth.

'Feast for me three times per year. Observe the feast of unleavened bread. Therein, according to my command, eat unleavened bread for seven days at the appointed time of the month Abib, because in the same month, you came out of Egypt. And do not show me your mouth empty-handed. And when the first yield of your sown farming is ready, then observe the harvest festival. And at the end of the year, when you gather the fruits of hard work and pile them, then celebrate the festival of gathering.

'Bringing the first part of the first produce of your land to the house of your God Jehovah. Do not cook a goat child in its mother's milk.

'You worship the Lord your God, then he will bless your grain water, and take away the disease from among you.

'In your country, no one will be conceived, nor will anyone be sterile; and I will complete your life.

'I will put my fear before you in the hearts of all those who will go among you, that I will ruin them, and I will show you the back of all enemies.

'I will not expel them from you in one year, lest the country become desolate, and the wild beasts will increase and cause you sorrow. I will keep removing them little by little before you till you have taken the country into full possession.

'I will give you control over the land from the Red Sea to the Philistines and from the wilderness to the Euphrates; I will also hand over the inhabitants of that country, and you will remove them from there.

'You neither make a covenant with them nor their Gods.

'May they not live in your country, lest they make you sin against me; Because if you worship their Gods, it will trap you.'

Then he said to Moses, 'You, Aaron, Nadab, Abihu, and the

seventy elders of the Israelites come up to the Lord and worship from afar. And only Moses comes near to the Lord, and others come with him. Do not come up.'

Then Moses went to the people and told them all the words of the Lord and all the laws. Then everyone said with one voice, 'We will obey all the things that the Lord has said.'

Then Moses wrote down all the words of the Lord. And got up early in the morning and built an altar under the mountain and twelve pillars according to the twelve tribes of Israel.

Moses took the Book of the Covenant and read it to the people. Hearing him, he said, 'We will do all that the Lord has said, and obey him.'

Then Moses, Aaron, Nadab, Abihu, and the seventy elders of the Israelites went up, and saw the God of Israel; under his feet, there was something like a sapphire platform, which was as clean as the sky.

The Lord said to Moses, 'Climb up the mountain to me, and stay there, and I will give you stone slabs, and the law you have written and I command you to teach them.'

Then Moses climbed up to the mountain of God with his tomb named Joshua.

And he said to the elders, 'You wait here till we come again to you; and listen, Aaron and Hur are with you; if anyone has a case, go to them.'

Then Moses climbed the mountain, and a cloud covered the mountain.

Then the glory of the Lord dwelt on Mount Sinai, and that cloud hovered over it for six days; and on the seventh day, he called Moses from the middle of the cloud.

And in the eyes of the Israelites, the glory of the Lord looked like a fierce fire on the top of the mountain.

Then Moses entered the middle of the cloud and climbed the mountain. And Moses stayed on the mountain for forty days and forty nights.

The Lord said to Moses, 'Tell the Israelites to bring an offering for me; take my offering from all those who wish to give it with their will.'

'And these things are to be taken from them: gold, silver, brass, blue, purple and red-colored cloth, fine linen, goat hair, scarlet-colored red rams, needle skins, acacia wood, oil for light, oil for consecration, and fragrance for the fragrant incense, onyx stone for ephod and peon, and gem for inlay.

'And they make a sanctuary for me, that I may dwell among them.'

Tabut-E-Sakina (Ark of the Covenant)

The Lord said to Moses, 'Whatever, I show you, that is a sample of the place of residence and all its belongings, according to that you make it.

'Make an ark of acacia wood; it shall be two and a half cubits in length, and an inch and a half in breadth and height. And it shall be plated in and out of pure gold, and upon the ark shall be made a gold fence. Cast four strings on its four legs, two strings on one side and two strings on the other side. And put the poles in the rings on both sides of the ark, so that the ark can be lifted on them. Let those poles be in the rings of the ark; And not be separated from it. And the testimony, I will give you to keep in the ark. Then make an atonement cover of pure gold; Its length is two and a half cubits, and its width is one and a half cubits. And to make two cherubs by casting gold, and making it cover both ends of the atonement. And make the cherubim and the atonement cover with its piece, and put it on both ends. And the wings of those cherubim should be spread over the top so that the covering of atonement is covered with them, and their faces will be face to face and toward the cover of atonement. And to cover the atonement on the ark, and the witness I will give you, keep it inside the ark. I will stay with you and meet you; I have to give you all the commands for the Israelites. I will talk to you about all of them from above the cover of the atonement and from among the cherubs, which will be on the ark of the witness.

'Then make a table of acacia wood; its length is two cubits, width one cubit, and height is one and a half cubits. Get it plated with pure gold, and make a gold fence around it.

'And make a track of four fingers wide around it, and make a gold fence around this track. And make four rings of gold and put them in the four corners of the table which will be on its four legs. They should be near the hard track, and let the baton houses work that the mains should be raised on their own. And make the poles made of acacia wood and put them to sleep, and lift the table from them. And make his casserole and pans, and spoon and pouring bowls, all of pure gold. And set the loaves of offering before me regularly on the table. Then make a lamp of pure gold. It should be made of gold, with its lamp, pies, and sticks; its wreath, knot, and flower, all be of one piece; and six branches coming out from its edges, three branches from one side of the lamp and three branches from its other side. Each cast should have as many as three blossoms, one each of knots, and one flower each, like an almond flower. This is the shape or form of the six branches arising from the lampstand; and like the almond flower in the stem of the candle, there should be four flowers with their respective knots and flowers. And out of the six branches of the lampstand, there should be a knot under each of the two branches, they should be made of the same piece with the lampstand. Their knots and branches should be of the same piece with all the candles, made of pure gold with the same piece made of pure gold. And make seven lamps; the lamps should be lit to light in front of the lamp. And all its masks and vase should be of pure gold. All of them, including all these things, should be made of pure gold. And be careful to make all these things similar to the model shown to you on this mountain.

'Then make ten curtains of the residence; get them made of battered linen and blue, purple and red cloth with cherubic cherubim. The length of each screen is twenty-eight cubits long and four cubits wide. All curtains should be of the same size. The five curtains are connected to each other; and then the five curtains are also connected to each other. Where these two curtains are added, put the blue-blue loop on both ends, putting fifty-fifty traps at both ends, so that they are face to face.

Make fifty gold bars; to connect the rings of the curtains to each other through the beams so that the habitat becomes one. Then to make eleven curtains of goat hair to give tent work over the residence. Each screen should be thirty cubits long and four cubits wide. Eleven curtains should be of the same size. And joining five curtains separately and then six curtains separately, and folding the sixth screen in front of the tent. And you should make fifty marks on the ends of the screen which will be mixed from outside and fifty marks on the ends of the other side which will be mixed from outside. And to make fifty poles of brass, and to attach the tentacles to the hooks, to make the tent join together so that it becomes one. And the hanging part of the curtains of the tent, that is, half the septum, hang on the back of the residence. And out of the length of the curtains of the tent, hang it here and there with one hand and hang it on both sides to cover the house. Then for the tent, make a veil of skins of red-colored rams and on top of that, there is also a veil of sues skins. Then make wooden planks of acacia to erect the residence. The length of each board is ten cubits and the width is one and a half cubits. Each of the planks should have two or two slings connected to each other. To make all the boards of the residence like this. And out of the planks that you will make for the residence, twenty planks are for the south side; and to make forty silver chairs under twenty planks, that is, two chairs for each of its tenons under one board. And on the other side of the residence, that is, to make twenty planks toward the north. And for them to make forty silver chairs, that is, there should be two chairs under each board. And to make six planks for the backside of the residence, toward the west. And in the back part to make two planks for the corners of the residence, and these should be two parts from the bottom and both parts should be mixed in one string each at the top. This is the form of both the boards. These should be for both corners. And there are eight planks, and they have sixteen silver chairs; that is, there should be two chairs under each board.

'Then to make wooden benches of acacia, that is, five for the planks on one side of the residence, and five for the planks on the other side of the residence, and five benches for the part of the residence which will be on the west side. The middle band which will be in the middle of the planks reaches from one end of the tent to the other. Then make the boards to be plated with gold, and their stringers who will work in the houses of the bands, also make them of gold. And erect the dwelling as shown to you on this mountain. Then make a middle curtain of blue, purple, and red color and the finely woven linen cloth. They were made with cherub works of embroidery. And hang it on four pillars of acacia covered with gold, their beadings are of gold, and they stand on four silver chairs.

'And hanging the middle curtain under the seedlings, carrying the ark of the testimony under its cover; therefore, that interstitial curtain should separate the holy place from the Most Holy Place for you.

'Then place the atonement cover over the ark of the witness in the Most Holy Place. And outside that curtain, lay the table on the north side of the abode. And place the lamp in front of the table on its south side. Then for the entrance of the tent, a curtain of blue, purple, and red was made, and a fine linen fabric made of embroidered cloth a curtain made. And make five pillars of acacia for this curtain, and make them covered with gold. Their links should be of gold, and five brass chairs should be made for them. Then make the altar of acacia wood, five cubits long and five cubits wide. The altar should be square, and three cubits in height. And make four horns on its four corners; they should be of the same piece, including it, and have it plated with brass. And to make its ashes, and shovels, and bowls, and thorns, and rings, its total goods are made of brass. And make a grating of its brass net; And to put four strings of brass on its four ends.

'And put that grating under the cornice around the altar so that it reaches the middle of the height of the altar. And make wooden sticks of acacia for the altar, and make them plated with brass. And the poles should be put in rings, that whenever the altar is raised, they should be on either side of it. Make the altar hollow with planks; be made as she is shown to you on this mountain. Then make the courtyard of the residence. For his south side, mix all the curtains of finely woven linen cloth so that his length is a hundred cubits; This is enough on the one hand. And make twenty pillars for them, and make twenty chairs of brass for them, and the pillars of the pillars and their strips should be of silver. And in the same way, the north side of the courtyard should also have a hundred cubits long, they also have twenty pillars and twenty pieces of brass for them also; the pillars and straps of those pillars should be of silver. Then there should be curtains of fifty cubits toward the west in the width of the courtyard, their pillars should be ten, and the food also ten. The width of the courtyard is fifty cubits on the east side. And there should be curtains of fifteen cubits on one side of the courtyard gate, and three pillars and three pillars. And on the other side, there should be curtains of fifteen hands, three pillars, and three eatables. Make a curtain for the courtyard gate, one which is made of blue, purple, and red cloth and the fabric of the fine linen made of twenty hands, the pillars should be four and the food also four. All the pillars around the courtyard should be connected by silver strips, their furrows should be of silver and the food should be of brass. The length of the courtyard should be one hundred cubits, and its width should be fifty cubits and its height should be five cubits, the pillars should be of brass. Like the residence, all the utensils and all the items and all its pegs and courtyards should be of brass.

'Then you command the Israelites, to bring to me the pure oil of olive extracted from the code so that the lamp will light up daily.

'In the tent of meeting, out of the middle curtain that will be in front of the witness, Aaron, and his sons keep the candle in front of the Lord from dusk to dawn. This method will always remain for generations of Israelites.

'Then bring among the children of Israel, your brother Aaron, and his sons named Nadab, Abihu, Eleazar, and Ithamar, that they may act as priests for me.

'And make holy clothes for your brother Aaron, for the sake of splendor and glory. And to all those who have wisdom in their heart, whom I have filled with the wisdom-giving spirit, you should order Aaron to make his clothes, that he should be holy for me to do the work of the priest. And the clothes that they will have to make are these, that is, Cinnabon; and the ephod, and the baga, the four-piece tunic, the priest's hat, and the waistband. These holy clothes should be made for your brother Aaron and his sons so that they should act as priests for me. And they should take gold and blue and purple and scarlet and fine linen. They make the ephod of gold, blue, purple, and red cloth, and the fine linen that is woven, which is the work of the skilled embroidery worker. And it should be connected in such a way that the ends of the two shoulders meet. And the decoction girdle on the ephod should have the same texture, and both of them should be seamless and made of gold and blue, purple and red, and of fine linen fabric. Then take two onyx gemstones and carve the names of the sons of Israel, six of them on one gem, and the other six on the other gem, according to the origin of the sons of Israel. Just as the work of the gem bearer is dug, so are the names of the sons of Israel carved on those two beads; and make them rooted in gold mines.

'And to put both beads on the shoulders of the ephod, they will be a gem to be remembered for the Israelites. That is, Aaron should put his name before the Lord on both his shoulders for remembrance. Then make gold bars, and make two chains of pure gold kneaded like cords; and to put the knotted chains in those mines.

'Then make the peon of justice also of embroidery work; to make gold like the ephod, and of blue, purple and red color, and fine linen of woven fabric. It should be square and double, and its length and width should be one second each. And inlay a four-row gem in it.

'The first line consists of rubies, Padma rags, turquoise, sapphire, and diamond in the second row; LA sham and Neelam in the third row; and in the fourth row there will be turquoise, onyx, and jasper. All these should be studded in gold mines. And the number of names of the sons of Israel should be as many as their names, that is, according to the number of their names, twelve names themselves, one name out of each of the twelve tribes is inscribed on each gem in such a way.

'Then put a chain of pure gold kneaded on the peon-like cords. And to put two pieces of gold in the peon, and put the two links on both ends of the peon. And to put both the golden chains in the two rings which are on the ends of the peon. And to put both the other ends of the two chains folded in front of him on the two shoulder ties of the inertial ephod in both mines. Then make two more pieces of gold on both ends of the peon, on the core of it which will be inside the ephod. Then make two more pieces of gold, except them, on the bonds of both the shoulders of the ephod, in front of them from below and near the joint of the ephod on the decoction of the sack. And the chaps should be tied with their rings in a string of ephods with blue ribs so that it should remain on the eagle's cut piece, and the chap should not be separated from the ephod. And each time Aaron enters the sanctuary, he will place the names of the Israelites above his heart on the court of justice, so that his remembrance before Jehovah will be constant. And you keep Urim and Thummim in the court of justice.

(Urim and Thummim were of stone. When an important issue arose in the nation of Israel, the high priest used them to do Jehovah's will in the same way as letters were cast. He put Urim and Thummim in the chest he used to go inside the holy camp.)

'Then make the robe of the ephod completely blue. It should be made of such that it has a hole in the middle to insert its head, and around that hole, there is a woven core like a hole in the armor so that it does not burst. And to make pomegranates of blue, purple, and red-colored cloth all around it in the circle below, and to put gold bells around them, that is, a gold bell and a pomegranate, then a gold bell and a pomegranate. Let it be around the circle under the robe. And Aaron should wear that robe while walking in the service, so that whenever he goes inside the sanctuary to the Lord or goes out, then his voice is heard, or else he will die. Then make a vaccine of pure gold, and in the raid, these letters should be dug in it, that is, "Holy to Jehovah."

'And tie it with a blue ribbon; which stays on the front of the turban. And it should be on Aaron's forehead, so that whatever the Israelites sanctify, that is, Aaron should bear the blame of all the holy things in the offering, and they will be on his forehead so that the Lord will delight in them.'

Moses stayed there forty days and nights with the Lord; And till then neither did he eat bread nor drink water. And he wrote the covenant words, the Ten Commandments, on those tables.

When Moses came down from Mount Sinai with both of his witnesses in his hand, rays were coming out of his face because of his conversation with the Lord, but he did not know that rays were coming out of his face. When Aaron and all the Israelites saw Moses seeing rays coming out of his face, they were afraid to go near him.

Then Moses called them; Aaron and all the leaders of the congregation came to him, and Moses began to talk to them.

After this, all the Israelites came, and he gave them all the commands that the Lord had given to him at Mount Sinai while talking with him.

Till the time Moses had spoken to them, he put a veil over his face. And whenever Moses went in front of him to talk to the Lord, then he kept taking off the veil till the time he left.

Then Moses said to the whole congregation of the Israelites, 'This is what the Lord has commanded.' Moses did according to whatever the Lord had given him. And on the first day of the first month of the second year, the residence was erected.

Moses erected the tabernacle and put its chairs on its planks, and put beams in them, and erected its pillars; he spread the tent over the tabernacle, and over the tent, he put on the veil; just as the Lord commanded Moses.

And he took the witness box and placed it in the ark, and put the poles in the ark, and covered it with atonement; and he brought the ark to the tabernacle, and put the middle curtain in the ark of the witness box of the hanging; just as the Lord commanded Moses. And he put the table in the tent of meeting, out of the middle curtain on the north side of the tabernacle, and they put bread on it before the Lord; just as the Lord commanded Moses. And he placed the candlestick in the tent of meeting in front of the table on the south side of the tabernacle, and he lit the lamps before the Lord; just as the Lord commanded Moses.

He placed the golden altar in front of the middle curtain in the tent of meeting, and burned incense on it; just as the Lord commanded Moses.

He put the curtain on the door of the abode. And placing the burnt offering at the entrance of the tabernacle of the tent of meeting, he offered burnt offerings and grain offerings on it; just as the Lord commanded Moses.

He put the pot between the tent of the meeting and the altar and put water in it for washing, and Moses and Aaron and his sons washed their hands and feet in it. And whenever they went to the tent of meeting or near the altar, they used to wash their hands and feet; just as the Lord commanded Moses.

Thus Moses completed all the work, the cloud covered the tent of meeting, and the glory of the Lord filled the tabernacle. And the cloud stayed on the tent of meeting.

Throughout the journey of the Israelites, it used to happen that whenever the cloud rose above the tabernacle, they traveled. And if it did not get up, they did not travel till the day it did get up. During the entire journey of the house of Israel, the cloud of the Lord was visible to the tabernacle by day, and the fire was visible to all of them in the same cloud at night.

'Be it any man from among the people of the house of Israel, or from among the foreigners who live among them, who will eat any kind of blood, I will turn against the one who eats the blood and destroy him from the midst of his people. Because the soul of the body lives in blood; I have given it to you to offer on the altar that you should atone for your life; Because blood is atoning for life. Therefore, I tell the Israelites that neither of you should eat blood, and the foreigner who lives among you should never eat blood.'

Then the Lord said to Moses, 'Tell the Israelites that I am the Lord, your God. Do not do according to the works of the land of Egypt in which you lived; not according to the works of the land of Canaan, where I take you; and do not follow the laws of those countries.

'To obey my own rules, and to obey my laws. I am your God, Jehovah. Therefore, you keep my rules and my laws constant; the person who obeys them will live because I am the Lord.

'None of you should go near any of his near family members to expose his body. I am the Lord.

'Do not expose your mother's body, which is your father's body. She is your mother, so you do not expose her body.

'Do not expose even the body of your stepmother; it is the body of your father.

'Whether her sister is real or her stepmother, whether she is born at home or outside, her body is not exposed.

'Do not expose the body of your granddaughter. Your foster sister, who was born to your father, is your sister so that her body is not exposed.

'Do not expose your aunt's body; because she is your mother's near family.

'Do not expose your uncle's body, that is, do not go to his woman; she is your aunt.

'Do not expose the body of your daughter-in-law, she is the woman of your son, so do not expose her body.

'Then unless a woman remains impure due to her season, do not go to her body to expose her body.

'Then do not become unclean by molesting the wife of your brother.

'Do not offer any of your children to offering them Lord, nor make your God's name impure; I am the Lord.

'The practice of sexual intercourse men to men is not to be followed; that is disgusting.

'Do not become impure by animal husbandry with any kind of animal, and no woman should stand in front of the animal to have sex with him; this is a very perverse act.

'Do not become impure by doing any such thing, because the nations that I am about to remove from you have become impure by doing such things; and their country is also defiled, so I punish them for their iniquity, and that country spews out its inhabitants.

'For this reason, you people keep my laws and rules, and no matter whether you are a foreigner and a foreigner living among you, none of you should do such a disgusting thing.

'Because all such abominations have been done by the people of that country who lived in it before you, because of that the country has become impure.

'Do this commandment which I have given you to obey, and do not follow any of the abominations which are prevalent before you, nor be defiled by them. I am your God, Jehovah.'

Then the Lord said to Moses, 'Tell the entire Bani Israel to remain holy; because I am your God, Jehovah, holy.

'You shall fear your mother and your father, and observe my sabbaths: I am the Lord your God.

'Do not turn to idols, and do not make statues of Gods; I am your God, Jehovah.

'When you make a sacrifice to the Lord, then make such a sacrifice that I will be pleased with you. His meat should be eaten on the day of sacrifice and on the second day, but what remains until the third day is burnt in the fire.

'If anything is eaten on the third day, it will be disgusting, and will not be accepted. And the one who eats it defiles the holy substance of the Lord, so he will have to bear the weight of his iniquity; that creature shall be destroyed from among its people.

'Then when you cut the fields of your country, do not cut every corner of your field, and do not choose the grain that has fallen from the cut field.

'And do not take the grain of your vineyard, and do not gather the fallen grapes of your vineyard; leave them to the poor and foreigners; I am your God, Jehovah.

'You shall not steal, nor to one another, neither to hypocrisy nor to lie.

'Do not make your God's name profane by taking a false oath in my name; I am the Lord.

'Do not darken one another, nor rob one another. Worker's wages should not stay with you the whole night. Do not curse the deaf, nor stumble before the blind. And to fear your God; I am the Lord.

'Do not be crooked in justice; neither favoring the poor nor seeing the face of the great man and contemplating it; To judge each other with religion.

'Do not turn around in your people by being a tattler, and do not tie tips to shed each other's blood; I am the Lord.

'Do not hold hatred toward each other in your mind; you must scold your neighbor, otherwise, you will have to bear the burden of your sin.

'Do not take revenge, nor hate your fellow brethren, but love one another as yourself; I am the Lord.

'You continue to follow my laws. Do not allow your animals to match animals of different races. Do not sow two kinds of seeds gathered in your field. And do not wear clothes made of linen and wool tincture.

'When you reach the land of Canaan and plant trees of some kind, then its fruits remain unpicked for you for three years. Therefore, some of them should not be eaten. And in the fourth year all their fruits be holy to praise the Lord. Then in the fifth year, you should eat their fruits, because they will give you many fruits; I am your God, Jehovah.

'You should not eat any meat with blood. Neither to sow nor to consider auspicious or inauspicious morals.

'Do not shave by keeping a circle in your head, nor shave your cheek hair.

'Do not rip off your body at all due to death, nor imprint it; I am the Lord.

'Do not pollute your daughters by making them prostitutes, lest the country is filled with horrors due to prostitution.

'Obey my sabbath, and continue to fear my sanctuary; I am the Lord.

'Do not turn to the exorcists and the spiritual seekers, and do not become impure because of them by searching for them; I am your God, Jehovah. Standing up in front of a braided one, and honoring the old, and continuing to fear your God; I am the Lord. If a foreigner stays with you in your country, do not grieve him.

'The foreigner who stays with you should be like a native to you, and love him like you; because you too were foreigners in the land of Egypt; I am your God Jehovah.

'Do not be crooked in justice, and in quantity, and weight, and measure.

'The true scales, the weights of religion, the true epha, and the inferiority of righteousness remain with you; I am your God, Jehovah, who brought you out of Egypt.

'Therefore, obey all my laws and all my rules and follow them continuously. I am the Lord.

'And do not follow the rituals of the people of the caste whom I remove from you; because those people who have done all these misdeeds, that is why I hated them.

'But I tell you that you will own their land, and I will make this country in which the streams of milk and honey flow, in your possession; I am your God, Jehovah, who has separated you from the people of other countries. Therefore, you can distinguish between pure and unclean animals and pure and unclean birds; do not be an animal or bird or some kind of creeping creature on the ground, which I have forbidden you to be impure, do not defile yourself.

'You remain holy to me; because I, Jehovah, am holy myself, and I have separated you from the people of other countries so that you continue to be mine.

'If any man or woman worships or exorcises the ghost, he must be killed. Stone him, their blood will fall on their own head.'

Then the Lord said to Moses, 'Tell Aaron that anyone who has any physical defect in your generation, may not come near to offer food to their God.

'No matter who is at fault, he should not come close, whether he is blind, whether he is clinging, whether he is fatigued, whether he has more parts, or his leg or hand is broken, or he is a hump or dwarf, or he has a defect in his eye, or the man's pimples are itching, or his eggs are deflated; Whoever has any physical defect in the lineage of Aaron the priest shall not come near to offer the burnt offering to the Lord. He who is guilty never comes near to offer food to his God. He should eat both the holy and the holiest food of his God. But because of his faults, he neither comes inside the veil nor near the altar, lest he profane my holy places; Because I am the Lord who sanctifies them.

Moses told these things to Aaron and his sons and to all the Israelites.

'Those who are blind or limb broken, or have itching, do not offer such things to the Lord, do not offer burnt offerings to the altar to the Lord.

'Any bull or sheep or goat whose part is more or less can be offered for voluntary sacrifice, but it will not be accepted to fulfill the vow.

'Whose eggs are buried or crushed or broken or cut, do not offer them to the Lord, and do not do the same thing in your country.'

Then the Lord said to Moses, 'When a calf or sheep or goat is born, it should stay with its mother for seven days; then from the eighth day onwards, he will be acceptable to the offering of the burnt offering to the Lord. Whether it is a cow, a sheep, or a goat, do not sacrifice him and his child in a single day.

'When you offer a sacrifice of thanksgiving to the Lord, do it in such a way that it will be acceptable. It should be eaten on the same day so that nothing of it should remain till morning. I am the Lord.

'Therefore, you obey and obey my commands; I am the Lord.

'And do not make my holy name unclean, because I must be considered holy among the Israelites; I am your holy Lord, who has brought you out of the land of Egypt so that I can be your God; I am the Lord.

'To observe a festival for the Lord for seven days every year. It should always be a method of your generation, that this festival should be observed in the seventh month. For seven days, you should live in the huts, that is, all the born Israelites should live in the huts, so that your generations may know that when the Lord was bringing our Israelites out of the land of Egypt, he made them stay in the huts; I am your God, Jehovah.'

And Moses told the Israelites the appointed time of the feast of Jehovah.

Then the Lord said to Moses near Mount Sinai, 'Tell the Israelites that when you enter the country that I give you. Sow your field for six years, and after six years sorting your vineyard and collecting the produce of the country; But in the seventh year, let the land merge with the sabbath; neither sow your field nor prune your vineyard.

'Do not reap what you grow in the harvested field by yourself, and do not break the vines of your uncultivated vine; because it will be the year of the supreme rest for the land.

'The produce of the rest of the land will provide food to you, your slave-maid, and the laborers and foreigners who live with you; your animals and all the animals in the country will also get food from all the produce of the land. Counting seven sabbaths, that is seven times seven years, this time of seven sabbaths will be forty-nine years.

'Then on the tenth day of the seventh month, that is, on the Day of Atonement, let the trumpet of the sound of shout be heard everywhere in all your country. And if you sell something to your brother-in-law or buy something from your brother-in-law, then don't make a fuss over each other.

'After the Jubilee, according to the number of years passed, buy it from each other, and sell it to you according to the yield of the remaining years.

'You should not disturb your brothers; fear your God; I am your God, Jehovah.

'Therefore, you obey my statutes, and follow my rules consciously; Because by doing this, you will live in that country fearlessly. The land will produce its products, and you will eat to your stomach, and you will live in that country fearlessly.

'And if you say what we will eat in the seventh year if we will neither sow nor gather the produce of our field?

'So, know that I will give you such a blessing in the sixth year, that the yield of the land will be useful for three years. You will sow in the eighth year, and you will eat from the old produce, and you will continue to eat from the old produce until the new year's yield is received.

'The land should not be sold forever, because the land is mine; and in it you will be foreigners and outsiders.

'If one of your brothers is a pauper and sells some of his own lands, then the nearest one of his relatives will come and redeem the sold part of his brother. If there is no redeemer for any man, and he has enough money to redeem his inheritance so that after counting the years from the time of his sale, he should repay the produce of the remaining years to the one who bought him; then he should be entitled to his own land.

'But if he does not have enough capital to be able to own it again, his sold land should remain in the hands of the purchasers till the year of Jubilee; and when it is left in the year of Jubilee, then that person becomes entitled to his own land again.

'If a man sells a house to settle in the city of the wall, then after selling it, he will be able to redeem it within a year, that is, he will have the right to redeem that person throughout the year. If he does not redeem throughout the year, then the house which is in the city of the wall remains of the purchaser, and in the generation, after generation, the offspring shall remain in it; And did not miss even in the year of Jubilee.

'But the houses of the villages without walls should be counted as the fields of the country; they will also be redeemed, and they may be released in the year of Jubilee. Nevertheless, the houses of the cities in the private part of the Levites should be saved by the Levites wherever they want.

'If a Levite does not redeem his inheritance, then the house sold that is in the city of his inheritance may be left in the year of Jubilee; because the portion of the Levites among the Israelites is their home in their cities.

'The grazing land around their cities should not be sold; because that will be their part forever.

'If one of your brothers becomes a pauper, and his condition becomes pity in front of you, then you should take care of him; he should be with you as a foreigner or a traveler.

'Do not charge interest or increase from it; to fear your God; so that your brother can live with you. Do not give him money on interest, nor give him food with the greed of profit. I am Jehovah your God; I have brought you out of the land of Egypt to give you the land of Canaan and to be your God.

'Don't make him serve as a slave. May he be with you as a laborer or a traveler, and serve with you till the year of Jubilee; then he shall go out from you with his children and return to his family and to the ancestral land of his fathers.

'Because they are my slaves, whom I brought out of the land

of Egypt; therefore, they should not be sold as slaves.

'Do not overpower him harshly. Keep on fearing your God, your slaves, and maids are among the nations around you and you must buy slaves and maids from them.

'From among the travelers who will live among you as foreigners, and also from their houses which are around you, and those who have originated in your country, buy slaves and maids from them; and they will be your part. You will also be able to possess your sons who will be after you, and they will be part of them. You should always take slaves for yourself but do not assert your authority harshly over your brothers who are Israelites.

'Then if a foreigner or a traveler becomes rich in front of you, and your brother becomes a pauper in front of him and sells himself in front of you to that foreigner or traveler or his descendant, then after he is sold he can be redeemed again. One of his brothers can rescue him, Or his uncle, or cousin, and any close family member of his clan can redeem him; or if he becomes rich, he can redeem himself.

'He should reckon with his purchaser from the year of his sale to the year of Jubilee, and the cost of his sale should be according to the number of years, that is, the price will be with him as in the days of the laborer.

'If there remain many years of the year of Jubilee, then from the amount of money he has bought, he should change the value of his redemption according to the number of years. Even if a few years remain in the year of Jubilee, he should calculate the value of his redemption according to the number of years, according to his master.

'He should be with his master as a laborer whose annual wages are fixed; his master should not assert his authority harshly in front of you. If he is not rescued from these customs, he should be left with his children and grandchildren in the year of Jubilee.

'Because the Israelites are my only slaves; they are my slaves taken out of the land of Egypt; I am your God, Jehovah.

'Do not make idols for yourself, nor do you erect any carved statue or pillar for yourself, nor do you set up carved stones to worship in your country; Because I am your God, Jehovah.

'Obey my sabbaths and fear my sanctuary; I am the Lord.

'If you follow my laws and obey my commandments, I will rain for you from time to time, the land will yield its produce, and the trees of the field will give their fruits. Even at the time of planting the vineyard, you will keep on stalking, and even at the time of sowing, you will keep on plucking the vineyards, and you will eat arbitrary bread, and you will be settled in your country. And I will give you peace in your country, and you will sleep and you will have no fear; And I will not let dangerous animals live in that country, and the sword will not go in your country. And you will drive your enemies away, and they will be killed by your sword. Five of you will chase a hundred and a hundred of you ten thousand; your enemies will be slain in front of you with the sword; and I will put my blessing on you and make you prosper and increase it, and I will fulfill my covenant with you, you will eat the old grain that is kept, and you will take out the old one even when new.

'I will maintain my abode among you, and my soul will not hate you. I will walk among you, and remain your God, and you will remain my people. I am the God of your God, who brought you out of the land of Egypt so that you do not remain slaves of the Egyptians.

'If you will not listen to me, and will not obey all these commands, and will obey statutes, and your soul will hate my judgments, and you will not obey all my commandments, but you will break my covenant, I will make you restless and suffer from tuberculosis and fever. I will also be against you, and you will be defeated by your enemies; your enemies will rule over you, and even when no one chases you, you will still run. And if you do not listen to me even after these things, I will chastise you seven times because of your sins, and I will break the pride of your strength, and make the sky like iron and the ground like brass for you; and your strength will be lost without cause, because your land will not yield its produce, and the trees of the field will not give their fruit.

'If you keep walking against me and do not obey me, then according to your sins I will inflict more and more trouble on you. And I will send forest animals among you, who will make you inanimate, destroy your domestic animals, and reduce your count, which will cause your roads to be deserted. Then if you do not correct these things with my correction, and keep walking against me, I will also go against you, and I will kill you seven times because of your sins. And I will bring you a sword that will completely reverse the covenant-breaking; when you go and gather in your cities, then I will spread the plague among you, and you will be handed over to your enemies.

'And I will scatter you among the nations, and will draw a sword behind you; your country will be heard, and your cities will be desolate.

These are the laws that the Lord had ordained for the Israelites through Moses on Mount Sinai.

The Lord said to Moses, 'By explaining to Aaron that whenever you light the lamps, then the light of the seven lamps is in front of the lamp.' That is what Aaron did, that is, according to the command that Jehovah gave to Moses, he lit the lamps to light up in front of the lamp. And the shape of the lamp was such that it was made of fabricated gold from found flowers; according to the model that Jehovah showed to Moses, he made the lamp.

Then the Lord said to Moses, 'Two silver trumpets should be made; use them to call the congregation, and to leave the camp. And when both of them blow up, then all the congregation should gather near you at the entrance of the tent of the meeting. If only one trumpet is blown, the chiefs who are the chief men of thousands of Israel should gather near you. When you people breathe and blow, then the cantonments of the east direction are departed. And when you breathe for the second time, then the camps of the south direction depart. He breathes and blows for his departure. When people have to gather and gather, they still blow but not by breathing. And the sons of Aaron, the priests, will blow those trumpets. May this matter always be your method for generations. And when you go out to fight against a persecutor in your country, then blow the trumpets with your breath, then the Lord, your God, will remember you, and you will be saved from your enemies. Blow those trumpets with your burnt offerings and peace offerings in your joyous day, and in your appointed feasts, and in the beginning of months. This will remind your God of you; I am your God, Jehovah.'

On the twentieth day of the second month of the second year, the cloud rose from the tent of the witness's residence, then the Israelites went out of the wilderness of Sinai, departing; the cloud stayed in a forest called Paran. The departure began according to the Lord's command that he gave to Moses.

First of all, the flag of the camp of the Jews departed, and the group went away; And his commander was Nahshon, the son of Amminadab. The commander of the tribe of Issachar was

Nethanel, the son of Zuar. The commander of the tribe of Zebulunites was Eliab, the son of Helon. Then the tabernacle was taken down, and the Gershonites and the Merarians who had taken up the tabernacle departed. Then the flag of the camp of Reuben traveled and they too formed teams. And his commander was Elizur, the son of Shedeur. The commander of the tribe of Simeonites was Shalumiel, the son of Surishaddai. The commander of the tribe of the Gadites was Eliasap, the son of Duel.

Then the Kohatis departed, carrying the holy things, until they reached the Gershonites and the Mararis erected the tabernacle of the tabernacle. Then the flag of the camp of the Ephraimites traveled, and they also made a team; and its commander was Elishama, the son of Ammihud. The commander of the tribe of Manassehites was Gamliel, the son of Padasur. The commander of the tribe of Benjamin was Abidan, the son of Gideoni. Then the flag of the camp of the Danes which was behind all the cantonments, departed, and they too formed a team; its commander was Ahiezer, the son of Ammishaddai. The commander of the tribe of the Asherites was Pagiel, the son of Okran.

The commander of the tribe of Naphtali was Ahira, the son of Enan. The Israelites departed accordingly and proceeded according to their respective groups.

Moses said to Hobab, the son of his father-in-law, Sueb, 'We travel to the place of which the Lord has said, "I will give it to you"; therefore, you also walk with us and we will do you good because Jehovah has spoken well of Israel.'

Hobab replied to him, 'I will not leave; I will return to my country and family.'

Then Moses said, 'Do not leave us, because you know where

we should camp in the forest, you do work for us. And if you go with us, then the goodness that the Lord will do to us we shall do with you.'

Then the Israelites departed from the mountain of the Lord and traveled for three days; in the course of those three days, the *Ark of the Covenant* of Jehovah went ahead of them, finding a resting place for them. When they departed from the place of the camp, then the cloud of the Lord overshadowed them throughout the day. As the ark departed, Moses used to say, 'Get up, O Lord, and let your enemies be scattered, and your enemies flee from you.'

And whenever he stayed, Moses used to say, 'Lord, come back to thousands of Israelites.'

There those people started murmuring and saying bad things; and started saying, 'Who will give us meat to eat? We remember the fish that we used to eat for free in Egypt, and those cucumbers, melons, and wheat, and onions, and garlic; But now, our life is terrified, nothing is seen here except this manna.'

Manna was like coriander, and its color was like pearl. People go here and there and collect it, and at night there was dew in the camp, and the manna fell with it.

So, the Lord listened, and his anger was kindled, and the fire of the Lord burned in the midst of them and started consuming one side of the camp. Then the people came to Moses and shouted; Moses prayed to the Lord, then the fire was extinguished.

The place was called Tabera, because the fire of the Lord was burning in their midst. Moses heard men of all the families weeping at the door of their tents; Moses also felt bad about them murmuring. Then Moses said to the Lord, 'Why do you treat your servant this badly? And what is the reason that I have not found favor in your eyes, that you have put the burden of all these people on me?

'Did all these people come from my own womb? Have I produced them, that you say to me, that just as a father carries a milk-laden child in his lap, so should I take these people in my lap and take them to the land for which they have pledged to give? Where do I get so much meat to give all these people? They are crying to me by saying this, that you give us meat to eat. I alone cannot handle all these people, because it is beyond my power. And if you have to treat me this way, then you have so much grace on me, that you take my life immediately, so that I will not be able to see my plight.'

The Lord said to Moses, 'Gather with me seventy men of Israel, whom you know are the elders and chiefs of their group, and bring them to the tent of meeting, that they may stand here with you. Then I will descend, I will speak to you there, and I will take some of the spirit that is in you, and they will carry the burden of these people with you, and you will not have to lift it alone.

'And say to the people, "Sanctify yourself for tomorrow, then you will have meat to eat; because you have cried while listening to the Lord, who will give us meat to eat? We were good in Egypt. Therefore, the Lord will give you meat to eat, and you will eat. Then you will not eat one day or two, or five, or ten, or twenty days, but you will eat it all month, till it starts coming out of your nostrils. And you should not be disgusted with him, because you have cried to the Lord who is in the midst of you, and in front of him, saying, why did we come out of Egypt?"'

Then Moses said, 'Of those, I am among, there are almost six hundred thousand; and you have said that I will give them so much meat, that they will continue to eat it all month long. Will all the sheep and cows be killed so that they get meat? Or should all the fish in the sea be gathered for them, so that they get meat?'

The Lord said to Moses, 'Has the hand of Jehovah become small? Now you will see whether my word that I have told you is fulfilled.'

Then Moses went out and told the people the words of the Lord; and seventy men from among their elders gathered and stood around the tent.

Then the Lord descended through the cloud and spoke to Moses, and took the spirit that was in him, and brought it among the seventy elders; and when that soul came in them, they started prophesying. But two human beings were left in the camp, one of which was named Eldad and the other was Medad, in them also came the soul; these too were among those whose names were written, but did not go near the tent, and they began to prophesy in the camp itself. Then a young man ran and told Moses that Eldad and Medad were prophesying in the camp.

Then Joshua, the son of Nun, who was Moses' minister and one of his chosen, said to Moses, 'O my Lord, Moses! stop them.'

Then a great wind came from the Lord, and it brought the quails out of the sea to the camp and around it, so that they hovered around two cubits on the ground for a day and a half here and there. And the people got up and gathered the quails all day and night, and throughout the day on the second day also; the one who collected at least the ten homer, and they spread them around the camp. The meat was in their mouths, and they could not eat it so that the anger of the Lord was kindled on them, and he killed them with a great blow. The place was named Kibrothattawa.

Then the Israelites departed from Kibrotahtawa and reached Hseroth, and stayed there.

Moses was married to an Ethiopian woman. Therefore,

Miriam and Aaron blasphemed him because of his marriage to a Kushi woman.

They said, 'Has Jehovah only spoken with Moses? Has he not spoken to us as well?' The Lord listened to them. Moses was much humbler in nature than all the people living around the earth.

The Lord suddenly said to Moses and Aaron and Miriam, 'All three of you come out to the tent of meeting.'

The Lord said, 'Listen to me, if there is a prophet among you, then I will reveal myself to him by seeing the Lord, or I will speak to him in a dream. But my servant Moses is not like this; he is faithful.' Then that cloud rose from the top of the tent, and Miriam had leprosy that turned white like snow. And Aaron looked at Miriam, and saw that she had become a leper.

Then Aaron said to Moses, 'My Lord, let both of us, who have sinned but also committed foolishness, not commit this sin on us.

'Do not let Miriam live like a dead person whose body comes down from her mother's stomach.'

So, Moses cried to Jehovah by saying, 'God, please heal her.'

The Lord said to Moses, 'If her father had spit on her face, would she not have been ashamed for seven days? So, she should be out of the camp for seven days after which she will be able to come back in again.' So, Miriam remained outside the camp for seven days, and the people did not leave until Miriam was able to come again.

They then departed from Haserot and camped in a forest called Paran.

There the Lord said to Moses, 'Send men to distinguish the land of Canaan, which I give to the Israelites; they shall be the chief men of the tribe toward their fathers.'

Upon receiving this command from the Lord, Moses sent men from the wilderness of Paran who were the leaders of all the Israelites.

His names are from the tribe of Reuben, Shammu, the son of Zakkur; Shaphat son of Hori out of the tribe of Simeon; of the tribe of Judah, Caleb son of Japunne; Yigal son of Joseph from the tribe of Issachar; of the tribe of Ephraim, Hosea son of Nun; from the tribe of Benjamin, Palati, the son of Rapu; from the tribe of Zebulun, Gaddiel son of Sodi; among Joseph's descendants, Gaddi son of Susie from the tribe of Manasseh; of Dan's tribe, Ammiel the son of Gamalli; out of the tribe of Asher, Satur son of Micael; of the tribe of Naphtali, Nahubi, the son of Vopsi; of Gad, Goel son of Maki.

These are the names of the men whom Moses sent to distinguish the land. And the son of Nun, named Joshua.

While sending them to distinguish the land of Canaan, Moses said, 'Go from here, that is, to the south, and go to the hill country and see that country, how is it? And look at the people in them, whether they are strong or weak, few or many, and what the country they inhabit is like, good or bad? And in what settlements they are inhabited, and the tentacles. We live or live in strongholds or forts, and how is that country, whether it is fertile or barren, and whether it has trees or not. And you must be courageous and bring some of the produce of that country, too.'

That time was the first of the grapevines. So, they went and took care of the whole country from the forest called Sean to Le Rehob, which is in the path of Hamat. They passed through the south, and went as far as Hebron; there lived Anakavanshi named Ahiman, Sheshai, and Talmai. Hebron was inhabited seven years before Egypt's Zoan. Then they went to a brook called Eshkol and broke a branch with a bunch of vineyards, and two men carried it away, hanging it on a stick; and they brought some of the pomegranates and figs as well. Because of the Israelites who had broken a bunch of vines from there, the place was named Ashkol Nala. After forty days, they returned with the distinction of that country. And in the place called Kadesh in the wilderness of Paran, Moses and Aaron and all the congregation of the Israelites arrived; conveyed to them and to all the congregation, and showed them the fruits of that country. He described Moses as saying, 'We went into the country you sent us; streams of milk and honey really flow in it, this is from its produce. But the inhabitants of that country are strong, and its cities are fortified and very large; we saw Anak dynasties there as well.

'The Amalekites inhabit the south; and the Hittites, the Jebusites, and the Amorites live in the hill country; and the Canaanites are inhabited on the banks of the sea on the banks of the Jordan River.'

But Caleb said to Moses with the idea of silencing the people, 'Let us go up and adopt that country; for we surely have the power to do so.'

But the men who went with him said, 'We do not have the power to conquer those people; for they are stronger than us.'

All the Israelites murmured at Moses and Aaron; the whole congregation began to say to him, 'Oh that we would have died in Egypt! Or would we have died in this forest!

'Why does Jehovah want to take us to that country to die by the sword? Our women and children will go in loot. Is it not good for us?' Then they said among themselves, 'Come, let us make someone our leader, and go back to Egypt.'

Then Moses and Aaron fell face to face with all the congregation of Israelites. Joshua, son of Nun, and Caleb, son of

Japunne, who were among the secretors of the country, tore their clothes.

The Israelites said to the entire congregation, 'The country that we have roamed around to distinguish is a great country.

'If the Lord is pleased with us, then we will deliver us to the country in which streams of milk and honey flow, and will give it to us.

'Only do this so that you do not rebel against the Lord; Do not be afraid of the people of that country, because they will be our bread; the shadow has gone away from them, and the Lord is with us; don't be afraid of them.'

Then the whole congregation shouted that they should be stoned.

The Lord said to Moses, 'How long will these people despise me? And how long will they not believe me even after seeing all my miracles? I will kill them, and will expel them from their inheritance, and will create from you a caste which will be bigger and stronger than them.'

Then the Lord said to Moses and Aaron, 'This evil congregation keeps murmuring about me, I have heard this murmuring of them. Therefore, tell them that the words of my life which you have heard about me, I will certainly deal with you accordingly, declares the Lord.

'Your dead bodies will be lying in this forest; and all of you who are counted as twenty years of age or older, that murmured at me, no one except Jephunne's son, Caleb and Nun's son, Joshua, would be able to go to the country about which I swore. But your children, about whom you have said that they will go into plunder, I will send them to that country; and they will know the country you have despised.

'But your dead bodies will be lying in this forest. And until your dead bodies melt in the forest, that is, for forty years, your children will wander in the forest, enjoying the fruits of your adultery. The number of days you went through that country, that is, forty days according to their count, instead of one day, you will bear the punishment of your iniquity for one year, for forty years, then you will know what my opposition is.

'I have said that the people of this evil congregation who have gathered against me will die in this forest; and, of course, I will do the same.'

Then Moses told these things to all the Israelites, and they started mourning a lot. They got up early in the morning and climbed to the top of the mountain, saying, 'We have sinned; but are ready now, and will go to the place the Lord has promised.'

Then Moses said, 'Why do you violate the command of the Lord? It will not be successful. The Lord is not among you, do not climb, otherwise, you will be defeated by your enemies.

'There are Amalekites and Canaanites before you, so you will be killed by the sword. You have left Jehovah and gone away, so he will not be with you.'

But they disobeyed and climbed to the top of the mountain, but the *Ark of the Covenant* of Jehovah, and Moses, did not leave the camp. Then the Amalekites and Canaanites who lived on that mountain climbed over them and continued to beat them up to Horma.

'The sin of the entire congregation of the Israelites, and also of the foreigner living among them, will be forgiven because it happened unknowingly to all the people.

'Then if a man sins in error, he shall offer a goat of one year for a sin offering.

'And the priest must make atonement before the Lord for a man who sins by mistake. Therefore, because of this atonement, that sin will be forgiven. Whoever does something by mistake, whether he is a native of Israel or whether you live as a foreigner among you, you should have only one system for everyone.'

Then the Lord said to Moses, 'Tell the Israelites that for every generation, you have to put a welt on the ends of your clothes, and put a blue lace on each side of the skirt; this will be such a welt for you, so that whenever you see it, then you will remember all the commands of your Lord; and you follow them, and you do not commit adultery as you have been doing, under the control of your mind and your eyes. But remember all the commandments of the Lord holy to your God and obey them.

'I am the Lord your God, who brought you out of the land of Egypt to be your God; I am your God, Jehovah.'

Then the Lord said to Moses, 'According to the houses of their ancestors, take one stick from each of their generals; write the names of the original men of each one of those twelve sticks, and write the name of Aaron on the stick of the Levites. Because each of the main men of the houses of the ancestors of the Israelites would have a stick. And put those sticks in the tent of meeting, before the witness, where I meet you. and the man I choose will bud in his stick; and the Israelites who murmur at you, I will take that murmur away from me.'

So, Moses said this to the Israelites; all their generals gave him one stick for themselves, according to the houses of their ancestors, so there were twelve sticks; Aaron also had a stick in those sticks. Moses placed those sticks in the tabernacle of the witness before the Lord.

The next day, Moses went to the tent of witness. Then, behold, the stick of Aaron, which was for the house of Levi, grew out of buds, and there were buds and flowers, and even ripe almonds. Took it near; they recognized their stick.

Then the Lord said to Moses, 'Put Aaron's stick again in front of the testimony, that it should be a mark for those who rebel, that you may stop the murmuring of those who continue against me in the future, lest that they die.' Moses did as per the command of the Lord.

In the first month, all the Israelites came to the wilderness called Sean, and lived in Kadesh; And there Miriam died, and was buried there.

There was no water available for the people of the congregation; so they gathered against Moses and Aaron.

And the people quarreled with Moses, saying, 'Oh, that we would have died only when our brothers died before the Lord! Why have you brought the congregation of the Lord to this forest, that we, along with our animals, die here?

'And why have you driven us out of Egypt to this bad place? Here, there is nothing of seed, or fig, or vine, or pomegranate, there is not even water to drink.'

Then Moses and Aaron went to the entrance of the tent of meeting before the congregation and fell on their faces, and the glory of the Lord was visible to them.

Then the Lord said to Moses, 'Take that stick, and you, along with your brother Aaron, gather the congregation and strike the rock in front of them, then it will give them water. In this way, you take water out of the rock for them and give them food for the people of the congregation and their animals.'

According to this command of the Lord, Moses took the stick before him.

Then Moses lifted his hand and hit the stick twice on the rock; And a lot of water came out of it, and the people of the congregation started drinking with their animals. But the Lord said to Moses and Aaron, 'You who did not believe me, and did not make me holy in the sight of the Israelites, so you will not be able to take this congregation to the land that I have given them.'

The well was named Mareeba, because the Israelites had quarreled with the Lord.

Then Moses sent messengers from Kadesh to the king of Edom. 'Your brother Israel says that you will know all the tribulations we have suffered, that is, our forefathers went to Egypt, and we stayed in Egypt for a long time; the Egyptians ill-treated our ancestors and also with us. But when we prayed to the Lord, he listened to us, and sent a messenger and brought us out of Egypt; so, now, we are in Kadesh city which is at your border. Let us go through your country. We shall not walk through a field or vineyard, and will not drink the water of wells; will go through the road, and neither will turn right or left until we are out of your country.'

But the king of the Edomites sent a message to him, 'Do not go through my country, or else I will go out to face you with a sword.'

The Israelites then sent to him, saying, 'We will walk by the road, and if we and our animals drink your water, we will pay for it, and nothing else, let us go out on foot only.'

But he said, 'You will not be able to come.' And Edom came out to confront with strength and a large army.

Thus, Edom refused to let Israel pass through their country. So, the Israelites turned from him.

Then the whole congregation of the Israelites traveled from Kadesh and came to a mountain called Hor.

At Mount Hor on the border of Edom, the Lord said to Moses and Aaron, 'Aaron will not be able to go among his people; to the land that I have given to the Israelites.

'Therefore, take Aaron and his son Eleazar to the Mount of

Hor; take off Aaron's clothes, and give these to his son Eleazar; Aaron will die.' Moses did according to the Lord's command; they climbed the Hor mountain in view of the whole congregation. Moses took off Aaron's clothes and dressed his son Eleazar, Aaron died there on the top of the mountain. Then Moses and Eleazar came down from the mountain.

When all the congregation of Israel saw that Aaron had died, then all the house of Israel wept for him for thirty days.

Then the Canaanite king of Arad, who lived in the south, heard that the Israelites were coming from the same route through which they had come, fought Israel, and took some of them captive. Then the Israelites made a vow to the Lord, saying, 'If you truly subdue those people, we will destroy their cities.'

The Lord overcame the Canaanites when they heard Israel's words; so they destroyed them along with their cities; with this, the place was named Horma.

Then they traveled from Hor mountain and took the path of the Red Sea to roam out of the land of Edom; and the mind of the people became very distraught because of the way.

So, they began to speak against God, and said to Moses, 'Why have you brought us out of Egypt to die in the wilderness? There is neither bread nor water, and our souls are saddened by this useless bread.'

So, the Lord sent strong venomous snakes into them, and many of the Israelites died. Then the people went to Moses and said, 'We have sinned, that we have spoken against Jehovah and against you; pray to Jehovah to take away the snakes from us.' Then Moses prayed for them.

The Lord said to Moses, 'Build a statue of a strong venomous snake and hang it on a pillar; then anyone who is trapped by a snake will see it alive.' So, Moses made a brass snake and hung it on the pole; then, whoever, looked at the bronze snake from the snakebite, survived.

Then the Israelites traveled and camped in Oboth. And traveled from Oboth and camped in Abarim, which is in the east in the forest in front of Moab. After traveling from there, they encamped in a place called Jared.

From there, they camped on the other side of the Arnon River, which flows into the wilderness and originates from the land of the Amorites; because Arnon lies between Moab and the Amorites, the border of the country of Moab.

Then they traveled from there to the haters. There is the same well about which the Lord said to Moses, 'Gather those people, and I will give them water.'

At that time Israel sang, 'O well, come up, sing about that well!'

The generals dug up, and the nobles of Israel dug up their trunks and sticks.

Then they traveled from the wilderness to Mattana, from Mattana to Nahiel, and from Nahiel to Bamot, and from Bamot to the valley which is in the plain of Moab, and to the end of Pisgah which is inclined toward Yeshimon. Then Israel sent messengers to Sihon king of the Amorites, saying, 'Let us pass through your country; we shall not turn and not go into a field or vineyard; we shall not drink the water of any well; and will go by the road until we are out of your country.' Yet Sihon did not allow Israel to pass through his country. Instead, he gathered all his Army and came out into the wilderness to confront Israel, and came and fought with them.

Then the Israelites killed him with the sword and passed over from Arnon to the Jabbok River, which was the border of the Ammonites. The boundary of the Amorites was firm.

So, Israel took all the cities of the Amorites and resided in them, that is, Heshbon and the cities around it. Heshbon was the city of Sihon, king of the Amorites. He fought the previous king of Moab and took away all his country from Arnon.

For this reason, the sorcerers say, 'Come to Heshbon, settle the city of Sihon, and be strengthened.'

'O Moab! Woe to you! The subject of the God of Kamosh was destroyed, he gave his sons a fugitive, and made his daughters maids of Emory King Sihon. We have toppled them, Heshbon has been destroyed up to Dibon, and we have also laid waste to Nopah and Medba.'

Thus Israel lived in the land of the Amorites.

Then Moses sent to spy out the city of Yazer; and they took his villages, and drove the Amorites there from that country.

Then they turned and started on the road to Bashan; Og, the king of Bashan, faced him, and he went out to fight with all his Army at Adrei.

Then the Lord said to Moses, 'Do not be afraid of him; for I will put him in your hands, including all the Army and the country; and do as you have done to Sihon, the king of the Amorites, Heshbon.'

Then they killed him, and his sons and all the people, so that none of them survived.

Then the Israelites traveled and camped near the Jordan River near Jericho in the Arabian plains. Balak, the son of Sippor, saw what Israel had done to the Amorites.

So, Moab was very afraid of them, knowing that the Israelites were many; even Moab was very distraught because of the Israelites.

Then the Moabites said to the Midianite elders, 'Now that party will lick all the people around us, just as the ox licks the green grass of the field.' At that time, Balak, the son of Sippor, was the king of Moab; he sent the messengers to Balaam, to the city of Pator, the land of the caste brothers of Balaam, the son of Bor, on the banks of the Euphrates, that they should call him, saying, 'Heard a band came out of Egypt, and the land covered them. They have gone, and now they have come before me and have settled. Therefore, come, and curse those people for my sake, because they are stronger than me, then it is possible that we may triumph over them, and we take them all from our country. Kill and remove; because I know that the one you bless is blessed, and the one you curse is cursed.'

He told them, 'Stay here tonight, and I will answer you according to what the Lord tells me.' Then the princes of Moab stayed at Balaam.

Then God came to Balaam and asked, 'Who are these men in your house?'

Balaam said to God, 'Balak, the king of Moab, the son of Sippor, sent me this saying, "Hear, the group that came out of Egypt has covered the land. Therefore, come and curse them for me;" It is possible that I can fight them out.'

God said to Balaam, 'Do not go with them; do not curse those people, because they are partakers of blessings.'

At dawn, Balaam rose up and said to the princes of Balak, 'Go away to your country; as the Lord does not command me to go with you.'

Then Moabi Hakim went to Balak and said, 'Balaam has refused to come with us.'

On this Balak again sent more princes, who were already distinguished and even more in count.

He came to Balaam and said, 'Balak, the son of Sippor, says, "Do not refuse any reason to come to me; for I will certainly do your great honor, and I will do whatever you tell me; so, come, and those curse the people for my sake".'

Balaam replied to Balak's servants, 'Even if Balak gives me his house filled with gold and silver, I cannot reverse the command of my God. So, now you guys tonight stay here, so that I know what else Jehovah says to me.'

God came to Balaam at night and said, 'If those men have come to call you, then you get up and go with them; but do what I tell you.' Then Balaam got up at dawn and tied a saddle on his donkey and went with the Moabite princes.

Because of his departure, God's wrath was kindled, and the angel of the Lord stood up blocking the way to oppose him. He was going on his donkey, and he had two servants with him. And the donkey saw the angel of the Lord standing in the path with a drawn sword in his hand. Then the donkey left the road and went to the field. Then Balaam hit the donkey so that he could return to the path.

Then the angel of the Lord stood in the street between the vineyards, which had a wall on either side. Seeing the angel of the Lord, the donkey was so close to the wall that Balaam's foot was buried against the wall; then he hit him again. Then the angel of the Lord stepped forward and stood in a narrow place, where there was neither a place to move to the right nor to the left.

Seeing the angel of the Lord there, the donkey sat down with Balaam. Then Balaam's anger erupted, and he hit the donkey with a stick. Then the Lord opened the donkey's mouth, and he said to Balaam, 'What have I done to you that you hit me three times?'

Balaam said to the donkey, 'You knocked me out. If I had a sword in my hand, I would have killed you right now.'

The donkey said to Balaam, 'Am I not the same donkey that

you have been riding from birth to today? Did I ever do this to you?'

He said, 'No.'

Then the Lord opened Balaam's eyes and saw the angel of the Lord standing in the path with a drawn sword in his hand. Then he bowed down and prostrated himself by falling on his face.

The angel of the Lord said to him, 'Why have you killed your donkey thrice? Listen, I have come to oppose you because you are doing evil tricks before me.

'And this donkey saw me and turned away from me thrice. If she had not turned away from me, I would surely have killed you by now, but would have left her alive.'

Then Balaam said to the angel of the Lord, 'I have sinned; I did not know that you were standing in the way to face me. So, now if you feel bad, I return.'

The angel of the Lord said to Balaam, 'Go with these men; but only say what I shall say to you.' Then Balaam went with the princes of Balak.

On hearing that Balaam was coming, Balak went to meet him in the city of Moab which is on the border of Arnon in that country. Balak said to Balaam, 'Didn't I send you with great hope? Then why didn't you come to me? Am I not worthy that you can really do your due?'

Balaam said to Balak, 'Look, I have come to you! But can I do anything now? Whatever God will put in my mouth, I will say the same thing.'

Then Balaam went with Balak, and they came to Kiriyathusoth. And Balak sacrificed oxen and flocks, and sent them to Balaam and the princes accompanying him. At dawn, Balak took Balaam to the high places of Baal, and from there, he was seen by all the Israelites.

The Israelites lived in the Shittim, and they molested the Moabite girls. When those women invited those people to the immolation of their Gods, then they ate and worshiped their Gods. Thus, the Israelites began to worship the God Baalpor. Then the anger of the Lord was kindled against Israel; the Lord said to Moses, 'Take all the generals of the people and hang them in the sun for the Lord, so that my furious anger will be swept away from Israel.'

Moses said to the judges of Israel, 'Kill all your men who have joined with Baalpor.'

When the entire congregation of the Israelites was crying at the entrance to the tent of meeting, an Israelite man brought a Midianite woman with him in front of Moses and his brothers' eyes. Seeing this, Phinehas, the son of Eleazar, the grandson of Aaron the priest, got up from the congregation and took a spear in his hand, and after the Israelite went to the camp, he also went in, and in the belly of both the man and the woman pierced the spear. At this, the disease that had spread among the Israelites came to an end.

Then the Lord said to Moses, 'Phinehas, son of Eleazar, grandson of Aaron the priest, who was jealous of me among the Israelites, has taken my rage away from them, that I did not burn them to an end.

'Therefore, tell me that I make a covenant of peace with him; and it will be a covenant of everlasting priesthood for him, and then for his offspring, because he was jealous of his God, and he made atonement for the Israelites.'

The Israelite man who was killed with a Midianite woman was named Zimri, son of Salu and head of his ancestral family from Simeon. And the Midianite woman who was killed was

Kozbi, the daughter of Sura, who was the head of a family of Midianite ancestors.

Then the Lord said to Moses, 'Persecute the Midianites, and kill them; because they cheat you by tricking the subject of knuckles and the subject of coziness.' Kozbi was the daughter of a Midianite chieftain and a caste sister of the Midianites.

Bani Israel's Counting

Then the Lord said to Moses and the son of Aaron the priest named Eleazar, 'Count all of them according to the houses of their fathers, who are eligible to wage war among the Israelites, who are twenty years old, or older, in the entire congregation of Israel.'

So, Moses and Eleazar the priest explained to them in the plains of Moab on the banks of the Jordan River near Jericho and said, 'Count the age of twenty and above, as the Lord commanded Moses and the Israelites at the time of their departure from Egypt.'

Reuben, the firstborn of Israel; had these sons; Enoch, from which the family of the Enochites came; and the pallu, who led to the clan of the palluies.

Hezron, the family of the Hezronites. These were the clans of the Reuben; who were counted forty-three thousand seven hundred and thirty men.

Pallu's son was Eliab. The sons of Eliab were Namuel, Dathan, and Abiram. These are the same Dathans and Abirams, who were the councillors; and at the time when the congregation of Korah had quarreled with the Lord, at that time they also had a quarrel with Moses and Aaron together in that congregation; and when those two and a half hundred people were consumed in the fire, that congregation disappeared, at the same time, the earth opened its mouth and swallowed them along with Korah; and they became a parable.

But the sons of Korah did not die. These are the sons of

Simeon from whom their families came; That is, Samuel, which led to the total of the Samuelites; and Jameen, that led to the family of the Jameenites; and Yakin, which led to a total of Yakinis; and Zerah, which led to the family of the Zerahites; and Saul, from which the Saulite family lived. These were the people of Simeon; of these, twenty-two thousand two hundred men were counted.

The sons of Gad from whom their families derived; that is, the Sapon, which led to the family of the Saponians; and the Haggis, which led to the Haggis clan; and Shuni, which led to a clan of zeros; and the Ozni, which led to the group of the Ozans; and Eri, leading to a clan of Eri; and Arod, which led to the family of the Aroids; and Arelli, which led to the group of the Arielites. These were the clans of Gad's clan; out of these, forty and a half thousand men were counted.

The sons of Judah were Er and Onan, but they died in the land of Canaan. And these were the sons of Judah from whom their families came out. That is, Shella, which led to the clan's total population; and the Perez that led to the clan of the Pereis; And Zerah, leading to a group of Zerahites. And these were the sons of Perez; That is, Hezron, the family of the Hezronites; And Hamul, which led to the family of Hamulites. These were all of the Jews; of these, seventy-six thousand and six thousand men were counted.

The sons of Issachar from whom their families derived; that is, Tola, which led to a total of Tollies; and Puvas, which led to the clan of Puvas; and Jashub, that led to the family of Jashubites; and Shimron, the family of the Shimronites. These were the clans of Issachars; out of these, sixty-four thousand three hundred men were counted.

These were the sons of Zebulun from whom their families

derived; that is, Sered, which led to a group of Serades; and Elon, from whom the family of the Elonites came; and Jahleel, which led to a clan of Jahleelites. These were the families of the Zebulunites; out of these, six and a half thousand men were counted.

Joseph's sons from whom his family emerged were Manasseh and Ephraim. These were the sons of Manasseh; that is, Makir, from which the family of Makiris came; and Makir was born to Gilead; and the family of the Gileadites went from Gilead.

These were the sons of Gilead; that is, EaJer, which led to the clan of EaJeris; and Helech, the family of the Helleites, and the Asriel, the family of the Asrielites; and Shechem, which led to the clan of Shechemites; and Shamida, which led to the clan of Shamidis; and Hepher, the family of the Hepherites; and he had only daughters, not sons of Hepher, the son of Hepher; the names of these daughters are Mahla, Nova, Hogla, Milka, and Tirsa. These were the clans of Manasseh; and those who were counted were fifty-two thousand seven hundred men.

These were the sons of Ephraim from whom their families derived; that is, the Shutellah, which led to the family of the Shutellahis; and the baker, which led to the family of the bakeries; and twigs which led to the group of twigs.

This was the son of Schuthelah; that is, Eran, which led to a total of Aranis. These were the families of the Ephraimites; out of these, two thirty-two thousand men were counted. According to their clans, these were the people of Joseph's clan.

The sons of Benjamin from whom their families derived; that is, the fiddle which led to the clan; and Ashbel, that led to the family of the Ashbelites; and Ahiram, which led to the Ahrimi's clan; Shapoopam, leading to a group of Shapoopamis;

and Hoopam, which led to a clan of Hoopamis. Bela had sons Ard and Naaman; And from Ard, the family of the Ardites, and from Naaman the family of the Naamanites. These were the Benjaminites according to their clans, and those who were counted were forty-five thousand six hundred men.

This was the son of Dan from whom his family originated; Of those who were counted among the Shuhamites, there were sixty-four thousand four hundred men.

These are the sons of Asher from whom their families derived; that is, the Imna, which led to the family of the Yiminis; Yishwi, which led to the Yishwyas' clan; and Bariya, leading to a total of haters. Then these are the sons of Beriah; that is, Heber, from which the family of the Heberites moved; and Malkiel, leading to Malkielians. And Asher's daughter's name is Serah. These were the families of the Asherites; of these, fifty-three thousand four hundred men were counted.

These were the sons of Naphtali from whom his family derived; that is, this cell, which led to the total of this cell; and the Goonies, which led to a total of Goonies; Yesser, which led to the family of the Yesserites; and Shillem, which led to a group of Shillemites. According to their clans, these were the families of Naphtali; And those who were counted were forty-five thousand four hundred men.

These were all those who were counted among the Israelites; that means there were six lakh one thousand seven hundred and thirty men.

Then the Lord said to Moses, 'To them, according to their count, that land should be distributed to be a part of it. That is, the total of which is more, more of those parts, and less of those which are less; each tribe should be given its share according to its numbered people. The country should be divided by letter.

The names of each tribe of the fathers of the Israelites may get their share as they come out.

'Whether, it is a part of many or a few, whatever parts are distributed, they should be distributed by letter.'

Then, there are those of the Levites who were counted according to their clans; That is, the family of the Gershonites, descended from the Gershonites; the group of the proverbs that came out of the proverb; and the clan of Merari who came out of Merari.

These are the total of the Levites; Libnas, Hebronites, Mushias, and Korahis and Kahat led to Amram, the wife of Amram's name is Yochabed, a descendant of Levi, who was born in the land of Egypt under the tribe of Levi; and she also gave birth to Aaron and Moses and his sister Miriam from Amram.

Aaron had Nadab, Abihu, Eleazar, and Ithamar. Nadab and Abihu died when they went to the upper fire in front of the Lord.

Of all the Levites who were counted, that is, all the men who were of one month or more, were twenty-three thousand; they were not counted among the Israelites because they were not given any part of the country.

Moses and Eleazar, the priests, who counted the Israelites on the banks of the Jordan River near Jericho in the Arabah of Moab, were counted among them.

But not one of the men of Israel who were counted by Moses and Aaron the priest in the wilderness of Sinai. Because the Lord said about them, 'They will surely die in the wilderness.' Therefore, none of them survived, except Caleb, son of Japunne, and Joshua, son of Nun.

Then the Lord said to Moses, 'Make your men with weapons for war that they climb upon the Midianites and take the revenge of the Lord from them. Send one thousand men from each tribe of Israel to fight.'

Then, of all the tribes of Israel, one thousand men from each tribe were chosen, that is, twelve thousand men armed with weapons for war. Those thousand-thousand men from each tribe.

Phinehas, the son of Eleazar the priest, was sent by Moses to battle, and Phinehas had in his hand the vessels of the sanctuary and the trumpets that were blown to breathlessness.

And according to the command that Jehovah gave to Moses, they fought the Midianites and killed all the men, leaving the remaining dead, they killed the five kings of Midian, AV, Rekem, Sur, Hur, and Reba; and they killed Balaam, the son of Bor, with a sword.

The Israelites imprisoned the Midianite women with children and plundered their cattle, their flocks, and all their possessions. And blew up all the cities in their residence and all the cantonments; then they, man and beast, took all the prisoners and all the plunder, on the banks of the Jordan River near Jericho, in the Arababa of Moab, near the camp, Moses and Eleazar came to the priest and the congregation of Israel.

Then Moses and Eleazar, the priests, and all the leaders of the congregation went out of the camp to welcome them. Moses became angry with the generals who returned after fighting, and said, 'Did you leave all the women alive?'

See, with the consent of Balaam, these women caused the betrayal of Jehovah to the Israelites about Por, and the Lord spread in the congregation.

'So, now kill every boy and every woman who has seen the face of a man. But all the girls who have not seen the face of the man, keep them alive for yourself.'

Moses went and told all the Israelites.

'Look, this command I give you today is neither hard for

you, nor far away. Nor is it in the sky, to say, "Who should ascend into the sky for us and bring it to us, and tell us that we should obey him?" Nor is it beyond the sea, that you should say, "Who should cross the sea for us, and bring it to us, and tell us that we should obey it?"

'But this promise is very close to you, in your mouth and mind, so that you can follow it. Listen, today I have shown you, life and death, loss and profit. Because I command you today, to love the Lord, your God, and to walk in his ways, and to obey his commands, laws, and rules, may you live and grow, and your God Jehovah bless you in the land you are going to possess. But if your mind wanders, and you do not listen, and wander off to worship the other Gods and start worshiping them, then I warn you today that you will undoubtedly be destroyed; and you will not be able to stay in that country for a long time, in which country you are going beyond the Jordan. Today, I make both heaven and earth a witness to you, that I have put life and death, blessing and curse before you; therefore, you should adopt life itself, that both you and your offspring may live; Therefore, love the Lord, your God, and obey Him, and cling to Him; because this is your life and long life, and by doing so you will live in the country that the Lord had sworn to give to Abraham, Isaac, and Jacob, that is, your ancestors.'

Moses also said to them, 'Today, I am one hundred and twenty years old, and now I cannot walk, because the Lord has told me that you will not be able to cross this Jordan River.

'Your God, who transcends you, is Jehovah; he will destroy those nations before you, and you will possess their country; and according to the word of the Lord, Joshua will pass ahead of you. And just as Jehovah has destroyed, Sihon and Og, the kings of the Amorites, and their land, in the same way, he will also do with all those nations. And when the Lord will deliver them to you, then do them according to all the commands that I have told you.

'Be bold and strong, do not be afraid or afraid of them; Because Jehovah is your God who walks with you; he will not deceive you and leave you.' Then Moses called Joshua and said to all the Israelites, 'Be courageous and strong with these people.'

Then Moses wrote this law to the Levitical priests, who were to carry the *ark of the covenant* of Jehovah, and handed it over to all the old people of Israel. Then Moses commanded them, 'At the end of seven years, that is, in the year of redemption, on the hut feast, when all the Israelites come to your Lord Jehovah in the place which he will choose, then read this law to all the Israelites. Recall. What men, what women, what children, foreigners within your gates, to gather all the people that they may learn by listening, and to guard in obeying all the words of this law, fearing the Lord your God, And their children who did not listen to these things also learn by listening, to keep the fear of the Lord your God, as long as you live in the land you are going across the Jordan to possess.'

Then the Lord told Moses, 'The day of your death is near; summon Joshua, and both of you come to the tent of meeting and present that I will command him.' Then Moses and Joshua went and appeared in the tent of meeting. Then the Lord appeared in that tent through the pillar of cloud.

Then the Lord said to Moses, 'You are about to fall asleep with your fathers; and these people will rise up and become adulterous after the foreign Gods of the land they will go to, abandon me and will break the covenant that I made with them.

'At that time, my anger will rage on them, and I will also discard them and hide my face from them, and these will become food; and many plagues and tribulations will come upon them, even at that time they will say, "Did these plagues not come upon us because our God was not in our midst?" When I deliver them to the land that I had sworn to give to their ancestors, and in which streams of milk and honey flow, and eat, they fill their stomachs, and they will become strong; then these strangers will turn to the Gods and worship them and will break my covenant by despising me.

'But still, when I have not reached them in the country about which I have sworn, I know what they are imagining; then this song will bear witness to them, because their children will never forget it.'

Then Moses wrote the word of this law from the beginning to the end.

Then he commanded the Levites carrying the ark of the covenant, 'Take this book of the law and place it near the ark of the covenant of your God Jehovah, that it may bear witness to you there. Because I know your rebellion and your persistence; behold, in spite of my being alive and with you, you have been rebelling against the Lord. Then why won't you do it even after I die! You gather all the old people of your tribes and your chiefs with me, that I may make them witness both the heavens and the earth against them by telling them these words. Because I know that after my death you will be completely spoiled, and you will leave the path in which I have led you; and in the last days, when you do the work which is evil in the eyes of the Lord, you will provoke it by worshiping the things which you have made, then you will be in a disaster.

'O sky! give ear, O earth! listen to the words of my mouth.

'My preaching will rain like rain, and my words will drip like dew, like mists on green grass, and shrubs on plants. I will preach the name of the Lord. Obey the glory of your God!

'He is a rock, his work is upright; all his ways are justice. He is the true God, he is not devious, he is righteous and upright. But the people of this race are crooked and skewed; they are spoiled, these are his sons. No, this is their stigma. Do you give this revenge to the Lord, O foolish and foolish people? Is he not your father who has bought you? He has made and stabilized you. Remember the days of ancient times, thoughts of generations after generations. Ask your father, and he will tell you. Question your old people, and they will tell you. When the Most High divided the individual parts of each race and settled the men separately, then he set the boundaries of the people of the country according to the number of the Israelites. Because the Lord's share is his subjects; Yakub is his inherited inheritance.

'He found him in the wilderness, and in the desert deserted and howling. He stayed around him and protected him, and kept him as a pupil of his eye.

'As the eagle hovers over its nest with its babies, it spreads its wings and picks it up on its wings. The Lord continued to lead him alone, and there was no other God with him.

'He rode him to the highest places of the earth, and fed him the produce of the fields. He licked her honey from the rock and oil from the flint rock.'

This is the blessing Moses gave to the Israelites before his death.

He said, 'The Lord came from Sinai, and rose from Seir for them; he showed his glory from the mountain of Paran, and came from the midst of millions of holy ones, with his right hand came forth volcanic methods for them. He surely loved the people.'

Moses said, 'O Lord, listen to Judah, and reach him to his people. He fought with his own hands, and you should be his helper against his adversaries.'

Then concerning Levi, he said, 'Thy Thummim and Urim are with your devotee, whom you have tested in the war, and with whom you have had a debate on the spring named Meriba; Bless the Lord, and his property. Receive the service of the hands; strike at the waist of his opponents and enemies, so that they cannot rise again.'

Then he said about Benjamin, 'That dear man of Jehovah will dwell in him fearlessly; he will overshadow him all day long, and he dwells between his shoulders.'

Then he said about Joseph; 'May his land be blessed by the Lord, that is, the precious substance and dew of the sky, and the deepwater that is beneath, and the ripe fruit of the sun, and the precious things that grow in the seasons, and the good things of the ancient mountains, and the precious things of the eternal hills, and the earth and the precious things which are filled in it, and the happiness of the one who lived in the bush. Regarding all of these, let blessings fall on Joseph's head, that is, on the moon of his head, which was separated from his brothers. They will call the people of the country to the mountain. They will pray there; because they will benefit from the wealth of the sea, and the precious substance hidden in the sand.'

Then he said about Gad, 'Blessed is he who increases silt! Gad remains like a lioness.'

Then he said about Dan, 'Dan is the child of a lion jumping from Bashan.'

Then concerning Naphtali, he said, 'O Naphtali, you who are satisfied with the pleasure of the Lord, and full of his blessings, you should possess the land of the west and the south.'

Then, regarding Asher, he said, 'Asher be blessed with sons. May he be dear to his brothers, and dip his foot in oil. Your shoes shall be of iron and brass, and so shall your power be in your day.

'There is no one like God, O Jeshurun, who rides in the sky to help you. The eternal God is your house, and beneath you are the eternal arms.

'And Israel is inhabited fearlessly, Jacob's fountain remains alone in the land of grain and new wine; there is dew from the sky above it. Blessed are you, O Israel! Who are like you, O saved people from the Lord? He is a shield for your help and a sword for your majesty; Your enemies will praise you, and you will trample their high places.'

Then Moses ascended from the plains of Moab to Mount Nebo, which is in front of the peak of Pisgah and Jericho; the Lord showed him all the land of Gilead, even the land of Naphtali, and the land of Ephraim and Manasseh, and the whole country of Judah to the west, and the south, and the valley of the city of Jericho, as far as Zoar, he showed it all.

Then the Lord said to him, 'This is the land which I swore to Abraham, Isaac, and Jacob that I would give to your descendants.'

'I have shown it to you, but you will not cross over and go there.' Then, according to the Lord's word, his servant Moses died there in the land of Moab, and they buried him in a valley in front of Bethpore in the land of Moab; Moses was one hundred and twenty years old at the time of his death; but neither his eyes were blurred, nor his virility was lost. Israelites wept for Moses in the Arabah of Moab for thirty days; then the days of weeping and mourning for Moses were over. Joshua, the son of Nun, was full of the spirit of wisdom because Moses laid his hands on him; the Israelites obeyed according to the command that the Lord gave to Moses.

And like Moses, there was no prophet in Israel with whom

Jehovah spoke face to face.

These halts occurred when the Israelites came out of the country of Egypt, led by Moses and Aaron. On the fifteenth day of the first month, he traveled from Ramesses; On the second day of Passover, the Israelites went out in fear of all the Egyptians,

1. The Israelites traveled from Ramesses and camped in Succoth.
2. And traveled from Succoth and camped in Etom, which is at the end of the forest.
3. And when they departed from Etom, they turned to Peahiroth, which is in front of Baal-sapon. And encamped in front of Migdol.
4. Then they traveled in front of Piheeroth, went through the sea, and went into the forest, and after walking for three days in the forest called Etom, they encamped in Mara.
5. They traveled from Mara to Elim and found twelve springs of water and seventy palm trees in Elim, and they encamped there.
6. Then they traveled from Elim and encamped on the banks of the Red Sea.
7. After traveling from the Red Sea, they encamped in the forest called Sean.
8. Then they traveled from the forest called Sean and camped in Dopka.
9. After traveling from Dopka, they camped in Aulish.
10. Having traveled from Aloosh they camped in Rapidim, they did not find drinking water there.
11. Then they traveled from Rapidim and camped in the forest of Sinai, traveled from the forest of Sinai and camped at Kibrotahtawa, traveled from Kibrothatawa and camped at Haserot, traveled from Haserot and camped at Ritma, traveled from Ritma and camped at Rimmonpres, traveled from Rimmonpres and camped at Libnah (Libya), traveled from

Libnah and camped at Rissa, traveled from Rissa and camped at Kahelata.
12. After traveling from Kahlata, they camped near Mount Sheper.
13. After traveling from Mount Sheper, camped at Harada, traveled from Harada and camped at Makhelot, traveled from Makhelot and pitched under, traveled under and camped at thirteen, traveled from thirteen and camped at Mitka.
14. They traveled from Mitka and camped in Hashmona.
15. And traveled from Hashmona, and encamped at Moseroth, traveled from Moserot and camped among the Yakanites, traveled from among the Yakanis and camped at Horhgidgad, traveled from Horhgidgad and camped at Yotbata, traveled from Jotbata and encamped at Abrona, traveled from Abrona and encamped at Aysongeber.
16. After traveling to Eshiongaber, they encamped in Kadesh in the forest called Sean.
17. Traveling from Kadesh, they encamped near Mount Hor, which is on the border of Edom.
18. Aaron died on Mount Hor on the first day of the fifth month of the forty-fifth year of the Israelites leaving Egypt. Aaron was one hundred twenty-three years old when he died on Mount Hor.

   The Canaanite king of Arad, who lived in the southern part of the land of Canaan, received news of the arrival of the Israelites.
19. Then the Israelites traveled from Mount Hor and encamped in Salmona, traveled from Salmona and camped in Poonon, traveled from Poonon and camped in Oboth, traveled from Oboth and encamped in the hills named Abarim, which are on the border of Moab.
20. After traveling through the hills, they encamped in Dibon,

traveled from Dibon and camped at Almondibalatham.
21. After traveling from Almondibalataim, they encamped in front of Nebo in the mountains called Abarim.
22. After traversing from the Abarim mountains, they encamped on the banks of the Jordan River near Jericho, in the Arabah of Moab.
23. From the Baytishimoth to the Abellashtim in the Arabah of Moab, they camped along the banks of the Jordan.
24. In the Arabah of Moab, on the banks of the Jordan River near Jericho, the Lord said to Moses.

'When you cross the Jordan into the land of Canaan, then expel the inhabitants of that country from their land; and destroy all their carved stones and molten idols, and destroy all their high places of idols worship. Take the country in your possession and live in it.'

God-Kings of Egypt

S.No.	King	राजा	Dynastic Period (BC)	
	First Dynasty 3100-2890			
1.	Narmer	नार्मर	3100	
2.	Aha	अहा	3100	
3.	Djer	जेर	3000	Narmer
4.	Djet	जेत	2980	
5.	Den	देन	2950	
6.	Anedjib	अनेदजिब	2925	
7.	Semerkhet	सेमरखेत	2900	
8.	Qa'a	का	2890	
	Second Dynasty 2890-2686			
9.	Hetepsekhemwy	हेतसेखमेव	2890	
10.	Raneb	रनेब	2865	
11.	Nynetjer	नीजेर	2795	
12.	Weneg	अनेज	2750	
13.	Sened	सेनेद	2725	
14.	Peribsen	पेरीसेन	2700	Khasekhemwy
15.	Khasekhemwy	खासेखमेव	2686	
	Third Dynasty 2686-2613			
16.	Sanakht	सेनेखेत	2686-2667	
17.	Djoser	जेसेर	2667-2648	
18.	Sekhemkhet	सेखेमखेत	2648-2640	
19.	Khaba	काब	2640-2637	
20.	Huni	हुनि	2637-2613	Djoser

#	Name	नाम	Years	
	Forth Dynasty 2613-2494			
21.	Sneferu	स्नेफेरू	2613-2589	
22.	Khufu	खूफू	2589-2566	
23.	Djendefre	जेडेफ्रे	2566-2558	Khufu
24.	Khafre	खफ्रे	2558-2532	
25.	Menkaure	मेनकुरे	2532-2503	
26.	Shepseskaf	षेप्सेसकां	2503-2494	
	Fifth Dynasty 2494-2345			
27.	Userkaf	उसेरका	2494-2487	
28.	Sahure	सहूरे	2487-2475	
29.	Neferirkare	नेफेरकारे	2475-2455	
30.	Shepseskare	षेप्सेसकारे	2455-2448	
31.	Raneferef	रेनेफेरेफ	2448-2445	Neferirkare
32.	Niuserre	नियेमेरे	2445-2421	
33.	Menkhauhor	मेनकुरे	2421-2414	
34.	Djedkare	जेडकारे	2414-2375	
35.	Unas	उनास	2375-2345	
	Sixth Dynasty		**2345-2181**	
36.	Teti	तेति	2345-2323	
37.	Userkare	उसेरकारे	2323-2321	
38.	Pepi-1	पेपी-1	2321-2287	
39.	Merenre	मेरेनरे	2287-2278	Teti
40.	Pepi-2	पेपी-2	2278-2184	
41.	Nitiqret	नीतीकरेत	2184-2181	
	Seven and Eighth Dynasty 2181-2125			
42.	Numerous Short Reigns			

#	Name	Name (Hindi)	Period	Image
	Ninth and Tenth Dynasty 2125-2025			
43.	Khety	खेती		
44.	Merykare	मेरीकारे		Merykare
45.	Ity	इती		
	Eleventh Dynasty 2125-1985			
46.	Intef-1	इंतेफ-1	2125-2112	
47.	Intef-2	इंतेफ-2	2112-2063	
48.	Intef-3	इंतेफ-3	2063-2055	
49.	Mentuhotep-1	मेंटहोतेप-1	2055-2004	Mentuhotep
50.	Mentuhotep-2	मेंटहोतेप-2	2004-1992	
51.	Mentuhotep-3	मेंटहोतेप-3	1992-1985	
	Twelfth Dynasty 1985-1795			
52.	Amenemhat-1	अमेनेमेत-1	1985-1955	
53.	Senusret-1	सेनुस्रेत-1	1965-1920	
54.	Amenemhat-2	अमेनेमेत-2	1922-1878	
55.	Senusret-2	सेनुस्रेत-2	1880-1874	Amenemhat
56.	Senusret-3	सेनुस्रेत-3	1874-1855	
57.	Amenemhat-3	अमेनेमेत-3	1855-1808	
58.	Amenemhat-4	अमेनेमेत-4	1808-1795	
	Thirteenth Dynasty 1795-1650			
59.	Hor	होर		
60.	Khendjer	हेजेर	1725	
61.	Sobekhotep-3	सोबेखोतेप-3		Khendjer
62.	Neferhotep-1	नेफेरहोटेप-1		
63.	Sobekhotep-4	सोबेखोतेप-4		
	Fourteenth Dynasty 1750-1650			
64.	A Series of	Minor	Ruler's	

#				
	Fifteenth Dynasty 1650-1550			
65.	Salitis	सेलीतिस	1650-1600	
66.	Khyan	ख्यान	1600-1555	
67.	Apepi	अपेपी	1555-1553	
68.	Khamudi	खामुदी	1553-1550	Khamudi
	Sixteenth Dynasty 1650-1550			
69.	Minor Hyksos rulers			
	Seventeenth	**Dynasty**	**1650-1550**	
70.	Intef	इंतेफ	1650-1600	
71.	Taa-1	ता-1	1600-1560	
72.	Taa-2	ता-2	1560-155	
73.	Kamose	कामोष		Intef
	Eighteenth Dynasty 1550-1295			
74.	Ahmose	अहमोस	1550-1525	
75.	Amenhotep-1	अमेंहोतेप-1	1525-1504	
76.	Tuthmosis-1	तुतमोसिस-1	1504-1492	
77.	Tuthmosis-2	तुतमोसिस-2	1492-1479	
78.	Tuthmosis-3	तुतमोसिस-3	1479-1425	
79.	Hatshepsut	हत्षेप्सुट	1473-1458	
80.	Amenhotep-2	अमेंहोतेप-2	1427-1400	
81.	Tuthmosis-4	तुतमोसिस-4	1400-1390	
82.	Amenhotep-3	अमेंहोतेप-3	1390-1352	
83.	Amenhotep-4	अमेंहोतेप-4	1352-1336	Tutankhamu
84.	Nefernefruaten	नेफरनेफरेत	1338-1336	
85.	Tutankhamun	तुतेनखामून	1336-1327	
86.	Ay	अयी	1327-1323	
87.	Horemheb	होरेमहेब	1323-1295	
	Nineteenth Dynasty 1295-1186			

#	Name	नाम	Years	
88.	Ramesses	रामेसेस-1	1295-1294	
89.	Seti-1	सेती-1	1294-1279	Seti-1
90.	Ramesses-2	रामेसेस-2	1279-1213	
91.	Merenptah	मेरेन्ताह	1213-1203	
92.	Amenmessu	अमेनमेसु	1203-1200	
93.	Seti-2	सेती-2	1200-1194	
94.	Saptah	सप्ताह	1194-1188	
95.	Tausret	तोसरेत	1188-1186	
	Twentieth Dynasty 1186-1069			
96.	Sethnakhte	सेतनाख्ते	1186-1184	
97.	Ramesses-3	रामेसेस-3	1184-1153	
98.	Ramesses-4	रामेसेस-4	1153-1147	
99.	Ramesses-5	रामेसेस-5	1147-1143	
100.	Ramesses-6	रामेसेस-6	1143-1136	Ramesses-2
101.	Ramesses-7	रामेसेस-7	1136-1129	
102.	Setepenre	सेटपेनरे	1136-1129	
103.	Ramesses-8	रामेसेस-8	1129-1126	
104.	Ramesses-9	रामेसेस-9	1126-1108	
105.	Ramesses-10	रामेसेस-10	1108-1099	
106.	Ramesses-11	रामेसेस-11	1099-1069	
	Twenty-First Dynasty 1069-945			
107.	Smendes	स्मेंदेस	1069-1043	
108.	Amenemnisu	अमनेमनिसु	1043-1039	
109.	Psusennes-1	सुसेनस-1	1039-991	
110.	Amenemope	अमिनेमोपे	993-984	Smendes
111.	Osorkon	ओसोरकों	984-978	
112.	Siamun	स्यामून	978-959	
113.	Psusennes-2	अमनेमनिसु-2	959-945	

#	Name	Name (Hindi)	Years	
	Twenty-Second Dynasty 945-715			
114.	Sheshonq-1	षेषोंन-1	945-924	
115.	Osorkon-1	ओसोरकों-1	924-889	
116.	Sheshonq-2	षेषोंन-2	890-889	
117.	Takelot-1	तकलोत-1	889-874	
118.	Osorkon-2	ओसोरका-2	874-850	
119.	Takelot-2	तकलोत-2	850-825	Sheshonq
120.	Sheshonq-3	षेषोंन-3	825-773	
121.	Pimay	पीमय	773-767	
122.	Sheshonq-4	षेषोंन-4	767-730	
123.	Osorkon-4	ओसोरकोंन-4	730-715	
	Twenty-Third Dynasty 818-715			
124.	Pedubastis-1	ऐदूबसतिस-1	818-793	
125.	Sheshonq-4	षेषोंक-4	780-777	
126.	Osorkon-3	ओसोरकों-3	777-749	Osorkon-3
	Twenty-Fourth Dynasty 727-715			
127.	Bakenrenef	केनरेफ	725-715	
	Twenty-Fifth Dynasty 747-656			
128.	(Kushite)	(कुसाइते)	747-656	
129.	Piy	पीय	747-716	
130.	Shabaqo	षबाको	716-702	
131.	Shabitqo	षबितको	702-690	
132.	Taharqo	तहारको	690-664	Shabaqo
133.	Tanutamani	तनुतामाने	664-656	

	Twenty-Sixth Dynasty 664-525			
134.	Saite	साइते	664-525	
135.	Nekau-1	नेकाऊ-1	672-664	
136.	Psamtek-1	समटेक-1	664-610	
137.	Nekau-2	नेकाऊ-2	610-595	Ahmose
138.	Psamtek-2	समटेक-2	595-589	
139.	Apries	एपरीस	589-570	
140.	Ahmose	अहमोस	570-526	
141.	Psamtek-3	समटेक-3	526-525	
	Twenty-Seventh Dynasty 525-404			
	First Persian Period			
142.	Cambyses	कैमबाईसिस	525-522	
143.	Darius-1	डेरियस-1	522-486	
144.	Xerxes-1	जरजीस-1	486-465	
145.	Artaxerxes-1	अर्तजरजीस-1	465-424	Darius-1
146.	Darius-2	डेरियस-2	424-405	
147.	Artaxerxes-2	आर्तांजरजीस-2	405-401	
	Twenty-Eighth Dynasty 404-399			
148.	Amyrataisos	अम्यर्तिओस	404-399	
	Twenty-Ninth Dynasty 399-380			
149.	Nepherites 1	नेफेरिट्स-1	399-393	
150.	Hakor	हाकोर	393-380	Hakor
151.	Nepherites 2	नेफेरिट्स-2	380-38	

#				
	Thirtieth Dynasty 380-343			
152.	Nectanebo 1	नेक्टानिबो-1	380-362	
153.	Teos	तेओस	362-360	
154.	Nectanebo-2	नेक्टानिबो-2	360-343	
		आर्टीजर्जीस	343-332	Darius 3
	IInd-Persian Period			
155.	Artaxerxes 3		343-338	
156.	Arses	-3	338-336	
157.	Darius 3	अर्सेस	336-332	
		डेरियस-3		Alexander The Great
	Macedonian Dynasty 332-305			
158.	Alexander The Great	सिकन्दर महान	332-323	
159.	Philip Arrhidaeus	फिलिप अरिहाइडस	323-317	
160.	Alexander IV	अलेक्जेंडर.4	317-305	
	Ptolemaic Dynasty		**305-30**	
162.	Ptolemy-I	टॉलेमी. 1	305-285	
163.	Ptolemy-II	टॉलेमी 2	285-246	
164.	Ptolemy-III	टॉलेमी. 3	246-221	
165.	Ptolemy-IV	टॉलेमी. 3	221-205	
166.	Ptolemy-V	टॉलेमी. 5	205-180	
167.	Ptolemy-VI	टॉलेमी. 6	180-145	
168.	Ptolemy-VII	टॉलेमी. 7	145-116	Cleopatra
169.	Ptolemy-VIII	टॉलेमी 8	117-107	
170.	Ptolemy-IX	टॉलेमी. 9	107-88	
171.	Ptolemy-X	टॉलेमी. 10	88-80	
172.	Ptolemy-XI	टॉलेमी. 11	80-51	
173.	Ptolemy-XII	क्लियोपेट्रा	-51	
174.	Cleopatra		51-30	

Printed in the USA
CPSIA information can be obtained
at www.ICGtesting.com
LVHW022113220724
786195LV00033B/214